# Digital Literacies

## Social learning and classroom practices

Edited by Victoria Carrington and
Muriel Robinson

UKLA

SAGE

Los Angeles | London | New Delhi
Singapore | Washington DC

First published 2009

Reprinted 2010

SAGE Publications Ltd
1 Oliver's Yard
55 City Road
London EC1Y 1SP

SAGE Publications Inc.
2455 Teller Road
Thousand Oaks, California 91320

SAGE Publications India Pvt Ltd
B 1/I 1 Mohan Cooperative Industrial Area
Mathura Road
New Delhi 110 044

SAGE Publications Asia-Pacific Pte Ltd
33 Pekin Street #02-01
Far East Square
Singapore 048763

UKLA Published in association with the United Kingdom Literacy Association (UKLA)

**Library of Congress Control Number: 2008942190**

**British Library Cataloguing in Publication data**

A catalogue record for this book is available from the British Library

ISBN 978-1-84787-037-7
ISBN 978-1-84787-038-4   (pbk)

Typeset by Dorwyn, Wells, Somerset
Printed in Great Britain by T.J. International, Padstow, Cornwall
Printed on paper from sustainable resources

**Mixed Sources**
Product group from well-managed
forests and other controlled sources
www.fsc.org  Cert no. SGS-COC-2953
© 1996 Forest Stewardship Council
FSC

# Contents

# Contributors

**Cathy Burnett** has had 20 years' experience of primary education, in schools, local authorities and at Sheffield Hallam University. She currently works with undergraduate and postgraduate students in initial teacher education. Her current research interests focus upon digital literacy and pre-service teachers' developing professional identity.

**Victoria Carrington** holds a Research SA Chair at the University of South Australia, where she is Professor in the Hawke Research Institute's Centre for Studies in Literacy, Policy and Learning Cultures. Victoria writes extensively in the fields of sociology of literacy and education, and has a particular interest in the impact of new digital media on literacy practices both in and out of school. Her research interests in the field of digital technologies and digital cultures have informed much of her work around early adolescents and youth. Her work has drawn attention to issues of text production, identity and literacy practices within the affordances of digital technologies and new media. Her contributions to the field have been recognized in the many keynotes and seminars she has presented at a range of national and international forums in Australia, Japan, Canada and the UK. Her work is regularly cited in the field of digital literacy and middle schooling and has been taken up by a range of national and international under/postgraduate education programmes. She is co-editor of the international journal *Discourse: Studies in the Cultural Politics of Education* (2003–present) and sits on the editorial boards of a range of journals including *Literacy* (UKLA), *Digital Culture & Education* and the *Journal of Early Childhood Education*.

**Julia Davies** is based at the University of Sheffield in the UK where she directs an online Master's programme in New Literacies, in Educational Research and the EdD in Literacy and Language. Her research focuses on the relationship between social learning and online digital practices; she is interested in looking at presentations of the self online; ways in which our notions of literacy are developing; thinking about definitions of text and the ways in which online affordances provide new ways of narrating ourselves and connecting with others. Among numerous chapters and papers, she has recently written a book with Guy Merchant, *Web 2.0 for Schools: Social Participation and Learning.*

**Clare Dowdall** is a lecturer in education at the University of Plymouth. She is currently engaged in doctoral research that explores pre-teenage children's digital text production and social identity work in online contexts. Her research interests pivot around the tensions that can be perceived between the formal curriculum for young children's education and their creation and engagement with texts in their own online spaces. In particular, she is keen to explore how children perform and negotiate their sense of self using digital texts as key platforms for the rehearsal, performance and negotiation of their social identities. Recently she has written about children's voluntary out-of-school text production, considering the features that may impact on this informal process.

**Rosie Kerin** is a lecturer in literacy in the School of Education and a researcher in the Centre for Studies in Literacy, Policy and Learning Cultures at the University of South Australia. Her key research interests include the integration of digital technologies and literacies in English/Literacy classrooms from the middle years of schooling through to tertiary settings, and implications for educators' professional learning and identities. Current projects include investigations into the pedagogical challenges and possibilities of Second Life and virtual worlds for tertiary education; and interventions in senior secondary schooling to engage and support students who have not met literacy benchmarks in the middle years of schooling.

**Kevin Leander** is Associate Professor of Education at Vanderbilt University in the USA. He was a secondary English and French teacher prior to returning to graduate school in English and Education. Leander's areas of interest include new media and literacies, literacy and space–time, and social theories of literacy. His recent projects involve studying the relations between the flows of new media and immigration, and studying how people learn across the space–time paths of their daily rounds.

**Guy Merchant** is a Principal Lecturer at Sheffield Hallam University, where he co-ordinates the work of the Language and Literacy Research Group. He has published numerous articles and book chapters on digital literacy and is co-editor of the *Journal of Early Childhood Literacy.* His research focuses on children and young people's uses of on-screen writing and how this can be incorporated into the school curriculum. He is co-author (with Julia Davies) of the book *Web 2.0 for Schools: Social Participation and Learning.*

**Muriel Robinson** is Principal and Professor of Digital Literacies at Bishop Grosseteste University College Lincoln. Her interest in this area grew out of PhD work looking at the ways in which children make sense of narratives in print and on television which suggested that there are many similar strategies being deployed. More recently, she has worked with Margaret Mackey developing the idea of an asset model of literacy, namely, a model which starts from the experiences, knowledge and skills that children have to draw on in any one situation rather than the more common deficit model which views popular culture as a negative influence on schooled literacy (with Mackey in N. Hall, J. Larson and J. Marsh (eds) (2003) *Handbook of Early Childhood Literacy*; with Turnbull in J. Marsh (ed.) (2005) *Popular Culture, New Media and Digital Literacy in Early Childhood;* with Mackey (2006) in Marsh and Millard's *Popular Literacies, Childhood and Schooling*). She has also explored the ways in which the next generation of primary teachers in England is being prepared and the extent to which they can be seen as Prensky's 'digital natives' (2001). Her work suggests that the students make a clear separation between the technologies of play and pleasure they use in their personal lives and the more functional uses of technologies they find in classrooms.

**Rebekah Willett** is a lecturer in media and cultural studies at the Institute of Education, University of London. She is also a researcher at the Centre for the Study of Children, Youth and Media. She has conducted research on children's media cultures, focusing on issues of gender, literacy and learning. In addition to publishing numerous book chapters and journal articles, she has co-written *Home Truths? Video Production and Domestic Life* (2009, University of Michigan Press) and co-edited *Digital Generations: Children, Young People and New Media* (2006, Lawrence Erlbaum), *Play, Creativity and Digital Technologies* (2008, Routledge) and *Video Practices: Media Technology and Amateur Creativity* (2009, Palgrave Macmillan).

# Series published in association with UKLA

The emphasis for all of the books is this series is on developing practical skills for teachers in literacy and language teaching, underpinned by accessibly presented theory and research. Dealing with topics of current and continuing interest, the books aim to inform all those concerned with the development of literacy: teachers, researchers and local authority professionals, as well as those involved in teacher education and continuing professional development.

Books in the series:

*Phonics: Practice, research and policy* Maureen Lewis and Sue Ellis (editors), 2006
*Visual Approaches to Teaching Writing: Multimodal literacy 5–11* Eve Bearne and Helen Wolstencroft, 2007.
*Desirable Literacies: Approaches to language and literacy in the early years* (Second edition) Jackie Marsh and Elaine Hallett, 2008.

The United Kingdom Literacy Association (UKLA) is a registered charity, which has as its sole object the advancement of education in literacy at all levels and in all educational settings in the UK and overseas. Members include classroom teachers, teaching assistants, school literacy co-ordinators, LA literacy consultants, teacher educators, researchers, inspectors, advisors, publishers and librarians.

UKLA provides a forum for discussion and debate through a wide range of international, national, regional and local conferences and publications. UKLA works with a range of government and non-governmental agencies on issues of national interest. The Association is also committed to the funding and dissemination of high-quality national and international research projects that include practitioner-researchers. This series of co-published titles with Sage Publications complements the range of in-house UKLA publications and provides a further opportunity to disseminate the high quality work of the association. In order to find out more about UKLA, including details about membership, visit: *http://www.ukla.org.*

# Introduction: Contentious Technologies

## Victoria Carrington and Muriel Robinson

Hong Kong, June 2008. This is an interesting place and moment to be writing the introduction to this particular text. We are surrounded by texts. As we walk the streets of Hong Kong the reality of Eric Sadin's (2007) *Times of the Signs* is visceral. Some texts are printed, some are digital, some are permanent, while others are ephemeral. Many texts, particularly the official signage that guides outsiders around the city, have English translations of various depth that draw on both British and American spelling conventions. In one large department store, words like attention and information are in English translation while the actual information on the sign remains in Cantonese. Laminated food menus throughout the city mix and match photographs with Cantonese and imaginative English translations. Marketing staff hand out flyers and tissues on every street corner; screens run the length of skyscrapers and move restlessly from advertising to news and weather and back again; every bar and every subway train has multiple screens playing news and different sporting events. At the same time, kerbside stands are bursting with printed newspapers, magazines and graphic novels, while graffiti and stickering – in both Cantonese and English – provide a parallel discourse on the city that adds to the cacophony of text. No one form of text reigns supreme; together they construct the multimodal textual landscape of the city.

Not so very long ago we would only have been discussing printed forms of text when we spoke of the textual landscape. In contemporary societies, we must now include texts created via digital technologies when we speak of the texts that cocoon us in our everyday lives and allow us to make our way through the city as we navigate our various social, political, cultural and economic obligations. Digital texts are ubiquitous. Digital texts are so embedded in the everyday fabric of this and most other societies that the very journey to our meeting place in Hong Kong would not be possible, or would at least have been very different and more challenging, without them. We flew in from the UK and Australia on aircraft resplendent with, and dependent upon, digital technologies. While on board we watched movies on our personalized digital screens, listened to music on our mp3 players, worked fitfully on our laptops and then played endless games on the screen. Now in Hong Kong, the international banking system uses digital technology to check our credit cards at hotel check-in, and we swipe our digital access cards to gain entry to the elevators and our rooms. Our Octopus cards (see www.hong-kong-travel.org/Octopus.asp) allow us to move through the city on the public transport system, sliding from subway to ferry to bus and back, and replace cash at all retail outlets along the way. Electronic route maps on the trains make it clear where we need to go, and during the journey we are surrounded by children and adults using phones, mp3 players, and hand-held games consoles to entertain, stay in contact, get information and create personal space. At every turn, digital technologies and texts keep us on the correct route, entertain us and connect the millions of us in Hong Kong, and around the world, in an intricate informational and multimodal web.

And yet, in many classrooms these devices and the texts produced with them are still perceived to be irrelevant, and even dangerous, in relation to children's learning and their development of powerful practices with text. To this day there remains a belief, entrenched in curricula and policy, that children and their learning should be quarantined from engagement with these texts and technologies, and should instead be taught and evaluated against a curriculum focused on print. As a consequence, an increasing number of the children and young people walking through the school gates each morning are required to leave behind an entire suite of competencies, practices and knowledge about digital technologies and digital text. Students are required to shift from a world replete with multimodal text, remixing and mashing, and fluid novice–expert relations, to a relatively unidimensional formalized context centred upon only one form of static text and structured by particular adult–child authority and knowledge hierarchies. These digital texts are no longer marginal or niche forms. Over the past decade they have rapidly become mainstream and powerful social texts that allow users and creators to engage in the gamut of social, cultural, economic and political activities required of effective and successful citizens. Prensky (2007) describes this shift from the everyday world saturated in digital technologies to the typical classroom as 'powering down'. Here Prensky is not only referring to the requirement that students leave digital technologies, particularly personal ones, at the gate; he is also referencing the different learning patterns, and levels of intellectual engagement and connectedness to the rest of the world, that students are required to adopt as they transition from outside to inside school each day. Prensky apparently wore a T-shirt with the text 'It's not ADD I'm just not listening' emblazoned across the front (see www.phillipdjwa.com/?p=51) when he gave the talk in which he coined the phrase.

We believe it is clearly evident that the range of text, and therefore the repertoire of literacy skills, required by the young in our society is expanding. At the same time, we also believe that print-based text is in no way endangered, but that it now interacts with digital technologies and multimodality to create new and more complex texts. In turn, these texts require new and more complex literacies – what Dowdall (in this volume) calls *critical digital literacies*. The tensions created, and professional rethinking required, when pursuing ways to work with the ever-developing technologies of our everyday lives, which remain contentious in terms of classroom practice and teacher education, produce what Watson (2000) and others have referred to as *wicked issues*. This book seeks to address these wicked issues, to show how research can inform our understanding of what children and young people do with these technologies, and to explore some ways in which teachers and teacher educators are seeking to work with the grain of digital culture to enrich the learning experience of their students.

We believe that new teachers must be prepared to teach in schools that are embedded in a world where technologies, particularly portable digital technologies, are changing the ways in which we make meanings and engage with each other. Some of these new technologies, particularly ones used at home or for social interaction, rest somewhat uncomfortably in schools and are still not universally assured of a place in classroom practice. This book seeks to identify the kinds of practices with, and masteries of, digital text that young people bring to classrooms from their out-of-school encounters with the contentious technologies of pleasure and utility available in our digital cultures. It therefore moves beyond an older model of either/or literacy. As we shall argue at greater length in the final chapter, there is no longer a place for a view of literacy that values *either* skills and practices with static print *or* those with digital text. The chapters in this book each make the case that children and young people require a *both/and* approach to print and digital text. Contemporary multimodal texts require what Leander (in this volume) calls a *parallel pedagogy* that weaves together the skills associated with digital and print texts to create and access meaning. Multimodal texts are neither print nor entirely digital; the literacies used in relation to these texts are already of the both/and form. It is time our classrooms became places where digital and print literacies come together to allow children opportunities to develop the skills and attitudes they will need to navigate complex urban sites and social forms.

This book enables new teachers, and those further into their career and returning to postgraduate study, to access the research currently being carried out into digital technologies. The book stresses the relevance for schools of research findings and suggests ways to develop new and more relevant pedagogies, particularly in relation to social learning, literacy and literate practices. The contributors to this book mark out a unique territory in literacy studies as they work together within a United Kingdom Literacy Association (UKLA)-sponsored special interest group to develop a coherent position on digital technologies and classroom pedagogies. Most have direct experience as primary or secondary teachers and are currently involved in teaching PGCE (Postgraduate Certificate of Education) and master's courses for teachers who are exploring these issues. They do so in a fluid and shifting institutional and policy context. Currently, teachers are being encouraged to develop professionally by undertaking relevant master's programmes, with the UK recently announcing its intention to move toward master's level qualifications for all teachers and many master's programmes worldwide encouraging participants to undertake small-scale action research on topics emerging from, and relevant to, their own professional situations. The English National Curriculum has been reviewed and the Literacy Strategy replaced with the Framework for Learning, which is more flexible and reflects greater awareness of the need to support children's learning across curriculum boundaries. However, it still pays significantly more attention to printed texts than to others. Australia is moving ever closer to a national curriculum and core literacy teaching methods, and in the meantime national literacy testing, which remains premised upon the primacy of print, is being embraced. At the same time, pre-service teacher education programmes are moving to incorporate the use of new media and digital literacies in recognition of the changing literacy needs of the community. The contributors show how the everyday lives of the students in our classrooms are inflected by a range of digital technologies that allow and encourage the production and use of an expanding palette of digital texts. Further, they explore the extent to which the uses and affordances of such technologies by young people in everyday life are aligned with the ways in which schools and teacher education programmes approach new digital technologies.

The chapters that follow are divided into four parts. The first three of these contain case studies by our contributors, each accompanied by a simple closing *download* to support early career teacher-researchers. These downloads summarize the key learning points, raise questions for reflection and point the less experienced reader to additional texts which may be helpful.

## Part A: Digital texts in and out of school

The initial section of this book considers issues related to the informal learning that many digital technologies promote. The emerging research is quite clearly demonstrating the power of informal learning networks established around the use of digital technologies; in particular the shifting expert–novice relations, but also the kinds of rehearsals, risks and collaborations that take place. The contributors explore examples drawn from the lifeworlds of children, young people and adults to demonstrate key principles of informal learning as they play out around these emerging technologies. Importantly, the chapters in this section foreground the value of these types of learning processes and their outcomes for young people's literacy practices.

A range of theoretical perspectives on this socially constructed model of learning is available to help us make sense of what we see. Way back in 1987 Janice Radway's study of women romance readers identified the way in which key members of any group can influence the practice of others. Fish's model of interpretive communities has been reshaped to recognize the dialectic relation-ship between younger members of society and the wider community in which they are growing up (Robinson, 1995). Lave and Wenger (1991) have developed a similar concept of communities of practice, also showing how new members to these communities both influence, and are influenced by, the experienced practitioners they encounter. Gee's (2004) notion of affinity groups is a further identification of the ways in which we are attracted to those who have similar interests and learn from each other as our engagement deepens.

Again and again in the chapters of this book, we will see how knowledge is socially constructed and mediated by the learners rather than simply absorbed unchanged from the expert, and this is particularly clear in this section when the contributors consider issues related to the informal learning that takes place around many digital technologies. The contributors explore examples drawn from the lifeworlds of children, young people and adults to demonstrate the principles of informal learning as they play out around these emerging tech-nologies. Readers are encouraged to reflect on how such instances of digital literacy practices might inform their own practice in different contexts and with different age groups through the interleaved reflection points which offer the less experienced researcher/beginner teacher support in recognizing the key messages of the chapters with regard to their own potential uses of technolo-gies in the classroom.

The section opens with Rebekah Willett's exploration of young people's digital productions as new sites of learning. Willett suggests that young people's digi-tal productions, particularly those emerging from out-of-school contexts, are often cited as instances of creative expression, new learning forms, sophisti-cated social networking and innovative practice. As such, educators are called on to examine these productions and the learning associated with them. This chapter analyses digital video production practices engaged in by seven young people outside schools, looking specifically at what and how these young peo-ple are learning. The chapter raises questions about how these out-of-school practices are being framed within research, and discusses challenges these prac-tices pose for educators.

Julia Davies then draws on research investigating online activities in a photo-sharing web 2.0 space, in order to look at ways in which playful collaboration helps individuals to learn from others through sharing and discussing content online. She suggests that the organizational templates that structure text-making within many online social spaces can help scaffold learning and develop creativ-ity. She begins to move us into the world of school learning by considering the multimodal aspects of digital texts, where the visual increasingly works in con-junction with the linguistic mode. Taking the view that the social and playful dimension of many Web 2.0 spaces develops collaborative ways of thinking and makes learning exciting, she suggests that using an online photo-sharing site in classrooms could serve as a useful tool suitable for guiding pupils in the thought-ful production and reading of digital texts in this technological age.

In the final chapter in this section, Clare Dowdall approaches school children's online out-of-school text production from an asset perspective and explores the masteries involved as they create texts. As these masteries are identified, the potential for developing parents', childrens' and educators' understanding of what critical digital literacy might involve, and the implications for classroom practice, are explored. Dowdall argues that the texts produced by young people in informal contexts should be viewed as highly purposeful, powerful and of consequence and, further, that the power of digital media requires response from educators and parents. She defines and argues the case for critical digital literacy.

## Part B: Changing literacies

Building upon this recognition of the power of informal learning and its link to powerful practices with digital text, this next part considers issues related specifically to classroom experience. It focuses more directly on the world of the classroom, with some very specific explorations of the ways in which web 2.0 possibilities such as wikis, blogs and virtual worlds are beginning to be used positively by some teachers. The contributors explore examples from primary classrooms to closely examine the practical implications of personal digital technologies for in-school learning. Readers are encouraged to reflect on how such instances of digital literacy practices might inform their own practice in different contexts and with different age groups.

Victoria Carrington opens this section by engaging with the issue of cultural shift, and focuses most particularly on the impact of wikis upon our notions of authorship, expertise and truth. She suggests that the ability to constantly change, edit, update and contest information on these sites brings to the fore the dynamic nature of electronic texts and, more interestingly, the contingent nature of information and expertise. The collaborative nature of wikis also requires active participation from a range of stakeholders and audiences, with the unavoidable concomitant tensions this entails, but also serves to demonstrate the increasingly participatory dimension of contemporary culture. Carrington argues that wikis, and the texts and communities produced via them, demonstrate the contingent, impermanent, and biased nature of information and 'truth' and, further, that they challenge many of the assumptions upon which contemporary literacy education has been based.

Julia Davies and Guy Merchant then continue with a chapter that explores the growing popularity of blogs and blogging as a way of self-publishing. Blogging involves relatively simple publishing tools that allow users – often at little or no cost – to publish on the web. Blogging constitutes a new and popular screen-based literacy practice (Lankshear and Knobel, 2003). Despite the deceptive impression of seemingly innocuous screen-based type that these online texts often give us, blogging presents the social affordance of textual connection with others online and offline, hyperlinks to information sources and other blogs, and the inclusion of different modes of communication. These dynamic connections are volatile and exciting because they challenge our notions of what it means to be writers and readers, and even unsettle our notions of what constitutes a text in online environments. The chapter will present ideas about ways that blogs can be used in schools to develop a range of literacy skills and to reflect with learners upon the affordances and constraints of blogs and blogging.

To conclude the section, Guy Merchant looks at how a group of primary school teachers in the North of England, with no previous experience of virtual worlds, engaged in planning and developing a three-dimensional (3D) online environment to enrich literacy provision in and between their own classrooms. Using Active Worlds, a client-server application that creates 3D virtual environments populated by users in the form of on-screen avatars, the project group worked to create an online space that would stimulate a wide range of literacy-based activity as children explored and interacted with each other. Navigational and communicational tools enabled participants to move around in virtual spaces such as streets, buildings and parks. Participants engaged in synchronous written conversations and sent each other electronic telegrams. The educational possibility for using such applications to create virtual communities (Rheingold, 1993), and to promote situated learning (Lave and Wenger, 1991), is well documented. However, research that investigates the learning potential of 3D virtual worlds in classrooms is still in its infancy. Merchant explores learning in virtual worlds from a number of different perspectives, and his chapter makes a detailed contribution to this area of research.

## Part C: Changing literacies, changing pedagogies

Our final section takes us into the world of teacher education. Clearly, for teachers to engage most productively with the full range of possibilities and affordances offered by digital technologies, and to learn how best to work with the potentially contentious technologies explored within this book, then both pre-service and post-qualifying teacher education needs to address the topic directly. The three contributors in this section have all begun to ask questions about pre-service teacher education in Australia, the UK and the USA. They question what capabilities and understandings the latest generation of recruits bring from their own personal encounters with digital cultures to their development and training as teachers, and how it is possible for the territory of curriculum development to engage with digital cultures. Burnett, Kerin and Leander draw upon their considerable experiences with undergraduate students to examine the ways in which digital texts and the practices around them are impacting on the work of early career teachers.

Cathy Burnett foregrounds the diverse experience with, and mastery of, digital literacy that student teachers bring with them to pre-service teacher education. Burnett argues that this diversity of experience is particularly significant given the conflicting discourses around technology and literacy in education.

Drawing from a qualitative study focusing on 10 primary school student-teachers, Burnett investigates these competing discourses and describes student-teachers' perceptions of the functions, processes, possibilities and values associated with digital literacy in and out of educational contexts. Sliding between analysis and practical advice, Burnett models methods that student-teachers might use to investigate the digital literacy experiences of students they work alongside in classrooms.

Rosie Kerin also focuses on student-teachers as they struggle with the tensions between changing literacy demands in their undergraduate programmes. In particular, Kerin notes that the steadily increasing expectation in the community about the digital literacy skills of educators does not mean that student-teachers, most of whom are school graduates of the past two decades, are universally digitally literate or confident with the use of digital technologies within educational contexts. This chapter examines the challenges, successes and problems associated with the introduction of a *digital portrait* as a mandatory assessment task for a literacy course within a teacher education programme. Student-teacher responses and reflections are analysed using a multiliteracies framework, and from this analysis recommendations are made for pedagogical and assessment practices that may enhance the inclusive and critical integration of digital literacies within teacher education.

Kevin Leander's chapter continues an engagement with and considers more closely the relationship between 'new' literacies and more conventional print-based literacies. Acknowledging that educators are under pressure to both preserve and teach conventional academic texts, Leander recognizes the power of out-of-school literacies that are increasingly premised upon mixing and remixing modes and mediums. Unpacking these tensions, Leander identifies four common stances on the relationship between these literacies: *resistance*, *replacement*, *return* and *remediation*. He makes use of the notion of remediation to describe his approach to a *parallel pedagogy*. Drawing from work with students, Leander describes the powerful negotiation that can be accomplished by teaching and working with both 'old' and 'new' literacy practices alongside each other.

## Part D: Interconnectivity

In the final chapter, we return as editors to the overarching themes of the book, identifying what has been learned and what remains to be explored. These themes include the nature of expertise and expert knowledge in a world of socially constructed learning and communities of practice, and the difficulties of holding to an either/or competitive model as opposed to a both/and stance which perceives all media, traditional and digital, as collaborating to support the meaning-making context.

From this re-examination of the underlying issues raised by the separate case studies, the chapter will move toward a synthesis of key themes for practitioners and those conducting practitioner and grounded research. It will do so using examples of the dissonance between the research findings that show us how children and young people engage with the world through digital technologies, and the ways in which such technologies are currently engaged by the formulation of education policy in this area.

The examples in the book bring together perspectives from a wide cultural, social and geographic area because they are drawn from the UK, the USA and Australia. At the same time, while exploring key issues from these diverse perspectives, the discussion has resonance for educators in all locations because digital technologies continue to cut across locational and temporal barriers. Readers will therefore have the chance to consider how the research they read about in the book sits alongside current policy in their own context, with regard to student age and the specificity of their education system, and to map out for themselves some ways forward for their own practice and research. The wide-ranging content provides many opportunities to expand thinking and professional practice.

# References

Gee, J. (2004) *Situated Language and Learning: A Critique of Traditional Schooling*. London: Routledge.

Lankshear, C. and Knobel, M. (2003) *New Literacies: Changing Knowledge and Classroom Learning*. Philadelphia, PA: Open University Press.

Lave, J. and Wenger, E. (1991) *Situated Learning: Legitimate Peripheral Participation*. Cambridge: Cambridge University Press.

Prensky, M. (2007) 'Handheld learning', keynote presented at the Handheld Learning Conference, 11 October, London. Accessed 28 August 2008 at www.slideshare.net/HandheldLearning/marc-prensky-keynote/

Radway, J. (1987) *Reading the Romance: Women, Romance and Popular Literature*. London: Verso.

Rheingold, H. (1993) *SmartMobs: The Next Social Revolution*. New York: Basic Books.

Robinson, M. (1995) *Children Reading Print and Television*. London: Falmer Press.

Sadin, E. (2007) *Times of the Signs: Communication and Information: An Analysis of New Urban Spaces*. Boston, MA: Springer.

Watson, D. (2000) 'Managing in higher education: the 'wicked' issues', *Higher Education Quarterly*, 54(1): 5–21.

# Part A

# Digital texts in and out of school

Increasingly, a fluid movement between print and digital text characterizes the lifeworlds of children and young people. The research described in this section demonstrates the power of learning communities established around the use of digital technologies in out-of-school contexts, with particular focus upon the shifting expert–novice relations and networking that using these technologies both requires and supports. Specifically, these chapters draw upon digital video production to examine: what and how young people learn in out-of-school contexts; the collaborative relationships that develop around the uploading and sharing of photos on flickr.com; and, finally, the online out-of-school digital literacy practices of early adolescents. Each chapter returns to the question of how educators might respond to literacy and learning evident beyond the classroom walls.

# 1

# Young People's Video Productions as New Sites of Learning

*Rebekah Willett*

## Introduction

Jacob, a twelve-year-old boy, shows me his latest video production: a skateboarding DVD. The title of the DVD, *Get Out*, refers to a sequence in the video when the skateboarders are chased away from a site where they practise their tricks. The DVD is presented with a printed covering, designed by Jacob, complete with his company name, Mimic Films. Playing the DVD reveals a stylized menu accompanied by the sound of skateboard wheels on pavement. As I click through the menu options, I am able to view carefully edited movies of Jacob and his friends doing tricks (or 'bailing'), each accompanied by a different style of music. Jacob tells me that he would like to run a skateboard company selling skateboards and accessories (including DVDs). He has already sold a few of his skateboarding DVDs, thanks in part to a teacher who was so impressed with the videos that he shared the DVD with the entire year group.

Readers of this chapter may find connections between this anecdote and their own experiences, as well as with other chapters in this volume: examples in which young people are producing digital media, connecting with peer cultures, being recognized by their teachers and projecting a future identity for themselves. One of my responses to Jacob was appreciation of his skills (both in skateboarding and digital media), his apparent ease with successfully performing an identity in both his peer life and his school career, and his learning of both skateboarding and media production, which involved hours of practice with no formal training.

It is easy to celebrate Jacob's learning. He is clearly a motivated learner, spending the hours needed to produce his DVD. His learning is embedded in his (skateboarding) culture, connects with his own experiences and helps him to make sense of the DVDs that he watches. He is reflecting on his consumption of skateboarding videos by critically analysing other works as well as his own. He evaluates and seeks to improve his own work: for example, he said that on this DVD he was unimaginative and always used slow motion for the jumps. He has a goal for his next project: to experiment with different music rhythms and tempos to match the style of skateboarding. For example, he plans to use slower music for long glides on the skateboard. As a learner in this context he has a positive identity aided in part by an interested teacher. He engages in constructionist learning (Kafai and Resnick, 1996), uses iMovie software to scaffold his learning, engages in non-linear forms of learning that are needed for his project and utilizes the Web to find answers to questions. Finally, his learning is part of his identity as a budding professional.

For educators, an example of learning such as this can be intriguing, and we might ask ourselves how the kinds of learning Jacob is doing in his home environment complement or connect with the kinds of learning he is doing inside schools. This chapter analyses learning specifically around camcorders and moving-image production occurring outside schools, and is based on interviews with young videomakers such as Jacob. Using literature on informal learning in relation to digital and participatory media cultures, the chapter raises questions about how we are to recognize and understand the skills and creative efforts of young people, and highlights challenges schools face as they consider current forms of media literacy that are needed by young people today.

## Digital cultures and new forms of learning

With learning of digital technologies taking place in informal settings such as homes, there has been considerable interest in contextualizing learning and looking at different styles and forms of learning (Coffield, 2000; Gee, 2004; Lave and Wenger, 1991). Toni Downes (1999) analyses approaches to learning taken by game players, identifying trial and error and learning-by-doing as dominant forms of learning. Arguing that game players are developing different approaches to learning, Downes writes, 'computing environments, through their interactivity, readily afford these approaches and therefore reinforce this pre-disposition towards exploratory modes of learning' (1999, p. 77). James Gee also focuses on video games, and discusses games as extraordinarily effective learning tools. In his book, *What Video Games Have to Teach Us about Literacy and Learning*, Gee (2003) outlines thirty-six learning principles which are inherent in people's game play: for example, he says that learning through game play is active, meaningful, multimodal, scaffolded, entails participation in social networks, encourages learners to take risks and allows for self-reflection. Gee argues that learning through game play is effective because skills are acquired in the context of an activity rather than through abstract exercises. As is evident when watching a child learning to play a video game, there are few times when children will sit down and be given step-by-step instructions by a tutor or instruction booklet. Similarly, Jacob described himself and his father learning to use iMovie to edit videos by experimenting with Jacob's skateboarding videos, through trial and error and, as his father said, through intuition.

Gee (2003) makes reference to Lave and Wenger's (1991) concept of *situated learning*, which frames learning as a type of social interaction rather than a cognitive activity. In Lave and Wenger's theory, members of a *community of practice* are brought together by a common activity centred on an area of knowledge. Because the community is built on common activity, learning involves relationships, the construction of identity in relation to the community and the development of particular practices (shared ways of doing things). Using the term *legitimate peripheral participation*, Lave and Wenger examine ways learners join a community of practice on the periphery and gradually move towards the centre as they become involved in the practices of that community. This is similar to the way Jacob has approached his skateboarding video: he first watched 'millions' of similar videos; he practised his own skateboarding (to make a skateboarding video the videographer also has to be on a skateboard); he hung out at skateboard parks, gradually moving to the centre areas to demonstrate his skills; and is now engaged in experimenting with recording and editing videos.

In relation to formal education, Lave and Wenger (1991) argue that there needs to be a shift away from the concept of an individual learner and that notions of mastery and pedagogy must be decentred: '[R]ather than learning by replicating the performance of others or by acquiring knowledge transmitted in instruction, we suggest that learning occurs through centripetal participation in the learning curriculum of the ambient community' (1991, p. 100). Gee's work (2004) similarly discusses the role of the social environment in learning, outlining the concept of *affinity* spaces as places where people with similar interests and goals come together to share knowledge. These concepts have been applied to learning related to digital technology in spaces such as forums and social networking sites, where young people immerse themselves in the language, skills and discourses of communities online (see Davies, this volume; Davies, 2006; Leander and Frank, 2006).

With high numbers of young people interacting online, questions are being asked about the skills and competencies that are being developed and the role of schools in providing opportunities to develop those skills. Jenkins et al. (2007) assert that participatory cultures build on traditional skills (literacy, research, critical analysis), but specific new media literacies are also developing. Rather than focusing on technological skills, new media literacy involves 'a set of cultural competencies and social skills' (Jenkins et al., 2007, p. 4). Jenkins et al. identify eleven new skills associated with online social environments, including appropriation, multitasking, collective intelligence, judgment, networking and negotiation. Importantly, although young people are developing new media literacies within participatory cultures, schools have a role in addressing these literacies. Jenkins et al. (2007, p. 18) outline three concerns that point to a need for educational intervention:

- How do we ensure that every child has access to the skills and experiences needed to become a full participant in the social, cultural, economic and political future of our society?
- How do we ensure that every child has the ability to articulate his or her understanding of how media shapes perceptions of the world?
- How do we ensure that every child has been socialized into the emerging ethical standards that should shape their practices as media-makers and as participants in online communities?

Some of these questions have been fundamental to those who have been involved in media education for many years (see Buckingham, 2003; Buckingham and Sefton-Green, 1993; Buckingham et al., 1995; Burn and Durran, 2007). These researchers see media literacy as involving social, cultural and analytical competencies rather than a set of skills to be learned by engaging with technologies. Media education, therefore, needs to draw on the cultural experiences of young people, recognize the barriers to participation, and provide students with skills to analyse and produce media in ways which extend and build on their existing knowledge. In relation to digital video production, studies have examined how new technologies support the development of understandings of production practices, making particular elements more visual (Buckingham et al., 1995; Sefton-Green, 2003). Furthermore, studies of practices in secondary schools in the UK have raised issues concerning not only how to teach but also what to teach in relation to digital production: for example, considering macro-level languages for different media genres, reflecting on issues of aesthetics, addressing different learning styles through different elements of digital media production, and considering when intervention is needed and when technology can scaffold learning (Burn and Leach, 2004; Reid et al., 2002). The ways these concepts are being understood, as young people experiment with different software packages in the home, is an increasingly important area of study as digital production practices become more commonplace.

## The study

The focus of this chapter is on young people's learning in relation to camcorders and related technologies (for example, editing software) in the home. Data discussed in this chapter come from a three-year project that is investigating the use of camcorders in the UK.[1] The data include individual interviews with contacts, such as Jacob, who belong to specific subcultures that use video, as well as interviews with users who do not see themselves as connected with particular cultures in terms of their video production. As such, the participants' orientation towards their media production practices varies, as does their investment in learning skills related to media production.

The participants for discussion in this chapter are seven boys aged 11 to 18, all located in the UK, who were contacted specifically because of their use of video (skateboarders and young videomakers), or who were part of a year-long study in which their households were given a camcorder. The household study participants had not had access to a camcorder before the project, but they all had access to a computer with editing software and most had internet access in their homes. The lack of female perspectives in this particular data relates partly to long-standing gendered constructions of, and orientations towards, technology: it was difficult to find girls who used camcorders, and many of the cultures which include video production are almost entirely male dominated (for example, skateboarding). We also found that when including a more female-centred culture, very often girls were unavailable for interviews via online contacts (possibly for safety reasons). In terms of the household study, in which twelve households participated, a majority of the girls were under age 8, and although some had tried videoing, they were not engaged with the camcorder in the way the older boys were. The participants in this research represent a mix of socio-economic groups, although there is a dominance of middle-class households. This might be expected considering the topic involves technology which is expensive to update (computers), and access to high speed internet access is required for full participation in many media production centred cultures.

The focus on learning was one part of the wider camcorder project, which also looked at the domestic context of the use of camcorders, and how wider cultural networks support, value and reward amateur videomaking. In terms of learning, we were asking about the processes that amateurs go through when producing videos. In relation to theories of learning and previous studies that analysed learning and digital cultures, as discussed in the previous section, we asked the following questions:

- What styles of learning can be identified?
- What are the participants' motivations for learning?
- How do they critique and seek to improve their own work?

These open-ended questions were posed in semi-structured interviews. The boys who were interviewed because of their specific uses of video were contacted through the video-sharing site, YouTube, or through personal contacts. Individuals in this group were interviewed face to face or over the phone, with follow-up questions via email. The boys whose families had been given camcorders were interviewed three times over the course of a year. These individuals were interviewed along with other family members who used the camcorder. The data were analysed in terms of emerging themes concerning learning, and are discussed in the following two sections: the first explores styles of learning, and the second examines motivation and audience feedback in relation to learning.

## What styles of learning can be identified?

Online communities that revolve around participatory media practices are often discussed as spaces in which people are striving to improve their work, where assessment is common and welcome, and where information is being shared (Gee, 2004; Ito, 2008; Jenkins, 2006). In spite of the extensive online discussions which took place around three out of the seven participants' productions, the data for the current study do not include examples of online learning communities that are operating with the same types of learning goals. This might be because the young people in this study are not concerned with techniques as much as they are with the ideas behind the videos. One participant specifically said that he was not aiming to produce a film of 'brilliant quality' and that he watches television and goes to the cinema if he wants to see professional filmmaking. In this participant's words, his interest in both producing videos and viewing videos on YouTube is 'not necessarily for how it's done but more for the content'. He goes on to comment about one specific video on YouTube, which he describes as 'interesting because of simplicity, how you make something simple and then put it on here and it gets like one million views, it's really effective'. This participant is highlighting the amateur aesthetic that contrasts with the aesthetic of high-budget films, and he is recognizing qualities of amateur film which specifically do not engage with professional filmmaking skills. This presents a challenge to researchers who discuss a 'pro–am (professional–amateur) revolution' and suggest that amateurs are challenging a pro–am divide by operating at professional levels, thus leading to a society in which 'there will be more innovation, deeper social capital and healthier democracy' (Leadbeater and Miller, 2004, p. 49). The young people in this study do not see themselves as professional amateurs, nor do they aspire to become professionals (only one of the interviewees was considering studying media production at university level).

Although perhaps not interested in acquiring professional skills, the participants clearly were learning skills that enabled them to produce videos. One of the significant changes in relation to learning with digital technologies is the scaffolding that current technology provides for learners. As one might expect, many of the young people to whom we gave camcorders were happy to experiment with the menus and buttons and to learn about the functions of the equipment through trial and error. The camcorder we provided has a joystick, which allows the user to navigate through menu options in a similar manner to interactions with computer games. This familiar environment encourages these young users to experiment with different menu options (including adding transitions to video segments, wind reduction, and adding effects such as sepia). Similarly, the ease of rewinding and watching a video on camera allows users to evaluate their video techniques. All of the young people in this study mentioned learning that arose from watching their videos and noticing problematic issues (for example, too much zoom, poor lighting, shaky camera). However, these are very limited uses of the camcorder, and one might ask how more advanced uses of the camcorder are learned.

Video-editing software is also scaffolding learning. With simple programs such as iMovie and MovieMaker bundled as standard software on computers, and free websites for video-sharing proliferating, producing and distributing an edited video has become an option that is easily available to many videomakers. When connecting the camcorder to a Macintosh computer, a dialogue box appears that asks users if they would like to make a Magic Movie. The program then proceeds to offer a selection of title formats and transitions, iTunes opens for users to select background music and, finally, users are asked how they want to share their movie (via email, DVD or on a website). After making these selections, the movie is downloaded from the camcorder, edited (that is, titles, transitions and music are added) and compressed to correct format. The software finishes by opening the appropriate application for sharing the movie (email, DVD burner or web browser). One might argue that this example is not about enabling production at all but, rather, disables users by hiding the process. However, I would suggest that for some users the interaction described here makes limited options visible, demonstrates the ease of using a particular program such as iMovie, and encourages users to explore the program further. Software companies have an economic imperative to scaffold learning in order to encourage users to continue using their product. Thus video games have different levels that get progressively harder as the player proceeds. Similarly, iMovie users can start with very basic editing and proceed to more advanced levels. Importantly, as our participants described, learning to use the software is intuitive. However, it is not just technical skills that new software scaffolds. Through visual layouts, digital technology also enables conceptual understandings of processes (for example, editing packages showing sound and image on two different strips) (see also Buckingham et al., 1995; Burn and Durran, 2007).

Although digital technologies may be enabling modes of learning such as trial and error, it is important to look at other modes of learning in relation to these technologies. A closer study also may provide information about the kinds of things that are learnt effectively through trial and error or technology enhanced scaffolding, and those that require more direct kinds of instruction. Although only one of the seven students in this study was enrolled in a media studies course at school, many of the young people had social networks that included older and more experienced technology users. For two of the boys in the study, interviews with their fathers revealed important scaffolding that was happening in the home as the young videomakers worked on their projects. Jacob's father worked with him to produce the skateboarding DVD using iMovie and, as Jacob describes, 'we kind of both learnt together'. Jacob's father is a graphic designer and artist, and is therefore familiar with digital technologies and design principles. Although he had not used iMovie before, as with any learner, his experience and knowledge contributed to his competent interaction with the program. Therefore, Jacob's experience learning iMovie was partly scaffolded by his father, who learnt side by side with him but also had other resources upon which to draw.

The youngest boy in the study discussed here (Ted, age 11) had more particular kinds of knowledge that were scaffolded by his father. Before being given a camcorder, Ted made videos using the video function on a stills camera. The videos he made are narratives, which often follow established movies or TV dramas. His father described how he directly taught Ted about particular concepts involved in filmmaking. For example, Ted was under the impression that his video needed to be shot in sequence, rather than shooting sections and then editing them together into the desired sequence. His father also taught him techniques of framing and storytelling within filmmaking, such as using perspective to make objects look bigger. Here we see conceptual work being taught more directly. As suggested by Burn and Durran (2007), 'children cannot be assumed to be "digital natives" (Prensky, 2001), who spontaneously know how to use digital technologies' (p. 168). Burn and Durran analyse exemplary practices in secondary school media studies classrooms, demonstrating the conceptual frameworks with which children engage when developing media literacy. However, although we have a growing number of examples such as Burn and Durran's, studies are still demonstrating a need to develop a more evidence-based curriculum in relation to media literacy, which charts the development of conceptual frameworks starting with primary and moving through to secondary school-aged children.

The role of the amateur and the scaffolding of learning both pose interesting questions for educators. If an amateur aesthetic is developing around videomaking, which is not about film grammar, production techniques or even legibility, then what is useful for young people to learn in schools about videomaking? Furthermore, if young people are learning editing skills on their own, what should teachers be doing?

More importantly, perhaps, are questions about digital divides. As can be seen with Jacob and Ted, social and economic resources are needed to participate in media production practices. We need to consider Jenkins et al.'s (2007) concern about ensuring that every child has access to the kinds of skills, knowledge, and learning increasingly valued within 21st century participatory media cultures. Who has responsibility for ensuring that the 'participation gap' does not widen? Schools are often looked to as one solution to the participation gap, by providing all pupils with access to technology. However, access to technology is never simple – schools have qualitatively different kinds of access, with physical, digital, human and social resources all impacting on the skills, knowledge and learning that can be expected (Buckingham, 2007; Seiter, 2005). Furthermore, the challenge of meeting individual needs arises when students such as those included in this study are in classrooms alongside students who have never touched a camcorder or editing equipment. Gender divides are also increasingly likely, if this study is anything to go by, with boys' cultures more likely to involve using technology to create finished products for display. If there are things to be learned from studying informal learning and digital cultures, perhaps it is the challenges these cultures pose for schools.

## Motivation and audience in digital videomaking

Similar to the learning involved in game play, as discussed by Gee (2004), motivation plays a key role in sustaining engagement with digital technology. For

Jacob, motivation to produce a movie about skateboarding comes partly from the fact that it is a subject with high status in his peer culture and that it is familiar to him as a consumer (he said he had watched 'millions' of skateboarding videos). The other interviewees also had specific motivations for producing a video, often connected with their media consumption and peer cultures. Some of the videos that were produced by the boys in the study include *Mislaid* (after the series, *Lost*), a new episode of *Doctor Who*, *The Brea Witch Project* (after *The Blair Witch Project*), *Wish You Weren't Here* (after the travel show, *Wish You Were Here*) and *Resident Evil 4* (after the movie and video game of the same name). Almost all of these productions were spoofs: a common style or genre of video found on the video-sharing site YouTube, as well as in comedy sketch shows on mainstream television. In addition to spoofs, the interviewees videoed football matches, music subcultures (particularly grime), school projects, and friends and family 'larking about'. In many of these cases, the interviewees were connecting with peer cultures and their own media consumption. This is not to say that learners always need to be motivated through connections to popular media cultures. Rather, as educators, we need to see what young people are already doing, so that we can build on their existing practices and knowledge, and identify barriers and enablers to new media literacies, in line with Jenkins et al.'s (2007) research discussed in the previous section.

One of the important developments for young people producing media is the ease of sharing their work with a potentially global audience. Work by Jenkins (2006) and Ito (2008) analyses how globalized fan networks are creating cultures in which consumers and producers are interacting in different ways, and where knowledge is being developed, shared and acknowledged. Ito's work, in particular, discusses the role of global networks in creating communities in which assessment of media productions is part of the ecology of the fan network. Similar to Gee's affinity spaces, these members of online communities have a shared interest in developing networks around a particular fan culture. In schools, teachers have long recognized the importance of audience, and have connected the motivation to produce, assess and improve work with an awareness of audience. However, not all work needs an audience. Some of the projects in the current study certainly were private and motivated by desires other than having an audience. For example, one participant said he keeps a video diary on his mobile phone and watches it back privately. Another participant made several narrative videos, based on *Jaws*, *Lost* and *Doctor Who*, but did not share these videos with anyone. These videos involved numerous takes, careful selection and creation of props, and detailed planning to create a correct sense of scale (for example, using toys in a fish tank as well as videos taken at the London Aquarium). Although he had the motivation to work through the production process, he had no desire to share his products. The motivation came from the process rather than the product.

Others in the study have large online audiences that would not have been possible before the advent of video-sharing sites. One group, The Bentley Bros, has a website devoted to their productions and includes a section of Bentley Bros fan art, links to four fan sites, and a forum with over 500 registered users and over 50,000 posts.[ii] On YouTube, their production *Resident Evil 4* has been viewed 270,000 times, received over 1,500 comments and at one point was number 56 in the all-time top-rated videos (in the games and gadgets category). This group is the most productive of the young people interviewed for this study, producing sixteen short videos, some of which are over sixty minutes long and are carefully scripted and edited. The role of digital technologies was key in the development of The Bentley Bros' productions, as Stuart Bentley explained in an interview for this study:

> We started filming around five to six years ago with a cheap old camera. They never went on the internet and were never edited, we just had some fun filming silly little clips around the house. It then became something a little more when we got a digital camera and editing software.

With the advent of video-sharing, the role of the audience has become an important motivator behind their productions, which are mostly parodic comedy sketches. Again, Stuart Bentley stated in his interview: 'We make spoofs purely to make the people watching laugh...and ourselves'. With the large fan base, as demonstrated by the evidence above, this group has a specific purpose for going through the production process and sharing their work online. However, video-making is not purely done for an audience. As indicated in Stuart's comment above, videomaking is also about having a laugh as a group of friends; this theme emerged in many of the interviews with young videomakers.

With millions of videos available online it is not easy to build a fan base and feedback is not always positive. Martyn Lomax, interviewee from a group called Random Loaf,[iii] specifically commented on the amount of 'flaming' on YouTube, indicating that many people see insults as the norm in terms of feedback: 'There's other people who just like to state their views, I found, they just don't like anything else that's created other than what they did.' As with any social environment, online spaces are embedded with power relations – there are superstars and bullies on social networking sites too. One of the interesting interactions to watch is how young people negotiate these power relations. Martyn said he sometimes views the profiles of the people who leave comments in order to understand why particular individuals who post insults might be offended by Random Loaf's videos. In one instance, in which a Random Loaf production made fun of a Rover Metro, Martyn traced an individual insult to someone who belonged to a Rover Metro enthusiasts club. In another instance, someone who was a fan of a particular football club was offended when the group made fun of the town in which the club was based, as Martyn explains: 'He found that we're slating his personal hobbies...it is down to the personal, the actual person who's writing the comments.' Martyn's comments indicate that making work public involves negotiation and considering an audience beyond one's peers. Random Loaf's work has been broadcast on terrestrial television, and Martyn's comments indicate his awareness of a wider audience beyond just the fans of Random Loaf, who might have the same interests and understandings as the producers. Martyn mentioned curbing the amount of swearing in the group videos and also commented on being aware of issues that might be sensitive to others. He explains that there are boundaries on what is appropriate to put on video-sharing sites: 'That's one of the things that I find you've got to be really careful of making videos, there's just this line that you can't cross.'

When lines are crossed producers sometimes enter into heated discussions. The Bentley Bros made a video that they described as 'a parody of chavs in Britain'.[iv] This video inspired an extensive online debate about 'chav' stereotypes. Many of the comments on the video (on YouTube and on the forum on the Bentley Bros' website) indicate that chav or similar subculture is seen to exist in different parts of the UK and in other parts of the world. However, one commentator critiqued the Bentley Bros' video by suggesting that the Bros were viewing chavs as a 'real' subculture, implying they should view chav as a stereotype. The commentator said it was sad 'that some thick, thick twats think these people are actually real'. Others criticized the Bentley Bros for reinforcing the chav stereotype. One person defended chavs by saying 'they're only a product of the system', and another said that the chav stereotype has 'been hyped and twisted by the media' and that the producers should 'stop whining and start realizing how bad the white working class have got it in the UK'. This second commentator addressed the Brothers as 'fucking middle class wannerbe scum bags', and this class divide also came through in comments about the actors' accents – there were several critiques of middle-class boys putting on working-class accents. In response to this debate, one of the members of the Bentley Bros posted the following:

> People stereotype, that's what they do. You aren't going to get past it ... You were baggy clothes, talk like a black guy when you're white, and you listen to rap? wigga? Maybe. Stereotyped as wigga? Yes. You have to live with it. People are ignorant enough to not get to know someone's personality and judge them on how they dress.[v]

In this statement, it appears that the Bentley Bros see the video as a chance to hold up the stereotype for critique. However, the ambiguity of their video leaves the Bros open to harsh criticism. This is a risk inherent in parody.

The data presented above show motivations for producing digital videos, as well as illustrating critical knowledge and negotiation skills that young people are developing as they engage with their audiences. As Jenkins et al. (2007) discuss, interacting in online spaces involves different kinds of resources, skills and competencies. These young people are developing an understanding of the way texts are read by different audiences, the power relations that are enacted in online discussions, different points of view and deeper understandings of cultural texts (for example, representations of chavs). As they engage in discussions which are immediate and relevant to them, and which relate to their cultural surroundings, these young people are learning how to negotiate their positions as readers and writers of media texts.

## Conclusion

I have suggested that young people in this study are successfully producing media, and in some cases they are engaging in discussions that involve conceptual learning and analyses of key media concepts such as representation. However, I have also suggested that we should not assume that young people are developing the media literacy skills they need, in relation to video production, simply by making movies with friends. The findings from this small-scale study demonstrate challenges for educators. Participatory media cultures sometimes include very productive learning environments. As we can see with Jacob and his skateboarding video, he is motivated and is learning new skills, assessing and improving his own work, making creative and aesthetic choices, and analysing media he consumes. Furthermore, he has a positive identity as a learner and sees his learning as related to his future. But Jacob did not learn everything on his own. He had scaffolding structures from the software that was supporting him, he had access to specialist equipment that supported his video-making (including a fish-eye lens to capture the skateboard video aesthetic), and his father was heavily involved in his learning. We also need to ask if Jacob is entering the participatory media cultures Jenkins discusses, by learning in new ways and developing new social skills and cultural competencies related to new media? Or is Jacob learning in more traditional ways with his father acting as a mentor? Finally, although Jacob found his video-making pleasurable in the same way as Gee (2003) describes the learning of video games, we need to ask if there might be things that videomakers need to learn even if they do not take pleasure in them now or in the future.

## Notes

i   The project Camcorder Cultures: Media Technologies and Everyday Creativity is funded by the UK Arts and Humanities Research Council (reference number RG/112277) and based at the Centre for the Study of Children, Youth and Media, Institute of Education, University of London.

ii   Retrieved 13 November 2007, from www.bentleybrosproductions.com

iii   Retrieved 13 November 2007, from www.randomloaf.com

iv   'Chav' is a derogatory slang term used to describe a stereotype of a particular youth subculture in the UK, associated with particular brands and styles of fashion, music, and attitudes (often considered to derive from American hip-hop culture). The stereotype is often connected with the white working class and is associated with poor education, resistance to authority and racist attitudes.

v   From the Bentley Bros Productions forum. Retrieved 8 May 2008, from www.setbb.com/bentleybrosprod/viewtopic.php?t=2064&mforum=bentleybrosprod

# References

Buckingham, D. (2003) *Media Education: Literacy, Learning and Contemporary Culture.* Cambridge: Polity.

Buckingham, D. (2007) *Beyond Technology: Children's Learning in the Age of Digital Culture.* Cambridge: Polity.

Buckingham, D. and Sefton-Green, J. (1993) *Cultural Studies Goes to School: Reading and Teaching Popular Culture.* Brighton: Falmer Press.

Buckingham, D., Grahame, J. and Sefton-Green, J. (1995) *Making Media: Practical Production in Media Education.* London: English and Media Centre.

Burn, A. and Durran, J. (2007) *Media Literacy in Schools: Practice, Production and Progression.* London: Paul Chapman Publishing.

Burn, A. and Leach, J. (2004) 'ICTs and moving image literacy in English', in R. Andrews (ed.), *The Impact of ICT on Literacy.* London: RoutledgeFalmer. pp. 153–79).

Coffield, F. (ed.) (2000) *The Necessity of Informal Learning.* Bristol: Policy Press.

Davies, J. (2006) 'Affinities and beyond: developing ways of seeing in online spaces', *E-Learning,* 3(2): 271–34.

Downes, T. (1999) 'Playing with computing technologies in the home', *Education and Information Technologies,* 4: 65–79.

Gee, J. (2003) *What Videogames Have to Teach Us about Learning and Literacy.* New York: Palgrave Macmillan.

Gee, J. (2004) *Situated Language and Learning: A Critique of Traditional Schooling.* London: Routledge.

Ito, M. (2008) 'Mobilizing the imagination in everyday play: the case of Japanese media mixes', in K. Drotner and S. Livingstone (eds), *The International Handbook of Children, Media and Culture.* London: Sage. pp. 397–412.

Jenkins, H. (2006) *Convergence Culture: Where Old and New Media Collide.* New York: NYU Press.

Jenkins, H., Clinton, K., Purushotma, R., Robison, A.J. and Weigel, M. (2007) *Confronting the Challenges of Participatory Culture: Media Education for the 21st Century.* The MacArthur Foundation. Retrieved 25 August 2008, from www.digitallearning.macfound.org/ atf/ cf/%7B7E45C7E0-A3E0–4B89-AC9C-E807E1B0AE4E%7D/JENKINS_WHITE_PAPER.PDF

Kafai, Y. and Resnick, M. (eds) (1996) *Constructionism in Practice: Designing, Thinking and Learning in a Digital World.* Mahwah, NJ: Lawrence Erlbaum.

Lave, J. and Wenger, E. (1991) *Situated Learning: Legitimate Peripheral Participation.* Cambridge: Cambridge University Press.

Leadbeater, C. and Miller, P. (2004) *The Pro–Am Revolution: How Enthusiasts are Changing our Society and Economy.* London: Demos.

Leander, K. and Frank, A. (2006) 'The aesthetic production and distribution of image/sub-jects among online youth', *E-learning,* 3(2): 185–206.

Prensky, M. (2001) *Digital Natives, Digital Immigrants.* Retrieved 25 August 2008, from www.marcprensky.com/writing/Prensky%20%20Digital%20Natives,%20Digital%20 Immigrants%20-%20Part1.pdf

Reid, M., Burn, A. and Parker, D. (2002) 'Evaluation report of the Becta Digital Video Pilot Project'. Retrieved 25 August 2008, from http://schools.becta.org.uk/upload-dir/downloads/page_documents/research/dvreport_241002.pdf

Sefton-Green, J. (2003) 'Informal learning: substance or style?', *Teaching Education,* 13(1): 37–51.

Seiter, E. (2005) *The Internet Playground: Children's Access, Entertainment, and Mis-educa-tion.* Oxford: Peter Lang.

# Download

## Key points

1. Although new technologies for media production often scaffold users' learning, a variety of social networks (peers, parents, relatives, online contacts, educators) are also needed to provide specific information and to build on conceptual frameworks.
2. Various digital divides are present (between households and schools as well as communities/nations), and these create challenges for schools, particularly when trying to meet individual needs.
3. Online spaces can provide powerful motivation and appreciative audiences, but they are also spaces embedded with power relations.

## In your classroom

1. As well as examining media studies concepts such as production, language, representation and audience, consider conceptual skills young people are developing when *producing* or responding to videos; the pleasures of, and motivations for, producing media (for both private and public consumption); and the ways young people are engaging as critical consumers on video-sharing sites.
2. Discuss the ways young people have developed audiences for their work, their role as an audience for other people's work and the different dynamics present on video-sharing sites.
3. Consider different digital divides that might be present in classrooms. What are the physical, digital, human and social resources that are impacting on young people's skills, knowledge and learning?

## Further reading

Buckingham, D. (2003) *Media Education: Literacy, Learning and Contemporary Culture.* Cambridge: Polity.

Burn, A. and Durran, J. (2007) *Media Literacy in Schools: Practice, Production and Progression.* London: Paul Chapman Publishing.

Jenkins, H., Clinton, K., Purushotma, R., Robison, A.J. and Weigel, M. (2007) *Confronting the Challenges of Participatory Culture: Media Education for the 21st Century.* The MacArthur Foundation. Available at www.digitallearning. macfound.org/atf/cf/%7B7E45C7E0-A3E0–4B89-AC9C-E807E1B0AE4E%7D/ JENKINS_WHITE_PAPER.PDF

# 2

# A Space for Play: Crossing Boundaries and Learning Online

*Julia Davies*

## Prelude

It is May 2006. I am in Manhattan, New York City, walking out of La-Delice Bakery on 3rd Avenue. I am carefully carrying a box of cupcakes, about to embark on a project, The Great Escape. It had all begun about a year earlier when someone (C-Monster, 2004) posted images of garish looking cupcakes to a photo-sharing website (Flickr.com). The cakes were huge cone-shapes, encased in lurid fondant icing, depicting faces with wide gaping mouths. The photographs attracted comments from many people; one suggested that the 'sugardudes' ... 'needed rescuing' (TroisTetes, 2005). Some commenters left links to images of similar cakes and others expressed how much they liked or disliked these 'creatures'. One person left an anecdote about how she always ate a frog cupcake on her birthday, and that these sugardude images had really brightened her day.

An eclectic, international mix of people thus exchanged biographical details, developing a cross-cultural joke; the focus on these ostensibly superficial and trivial novelty items drew people together across cultural and geographical divides. The 'in-joke' quickly developed among disparately placed individuals, and a social history developed among participants who then progressed their online connectivity, looking at each others' wider (non-sugardude) photo-collections. I read many comments on the sugardude images (also looking at many more on Flickr) and gradually learnt about the people who played with the idea of the sugardudes. A holiday in New York eventually led to a meeting with C-Monster and other online contacts; when the escape of the 'prisoner sugardudes' from the bakery would be executed and photographically recorded. After buying around a dozen cakes we took many photographs of the confectionery in a staged bakery escape, albeit with one casualty run-over by a yellow cab. Using cardboard cut-outs and cocktail sticks, we fashioned a 'statue of liberty' as well as little placards for the 'dudes' to 'carry'. The result was several series of images

27

arranged in online digital slideshows including a 'meta-series' of us taking the photographs. Figure 2.1 shows an example of an image from one series.

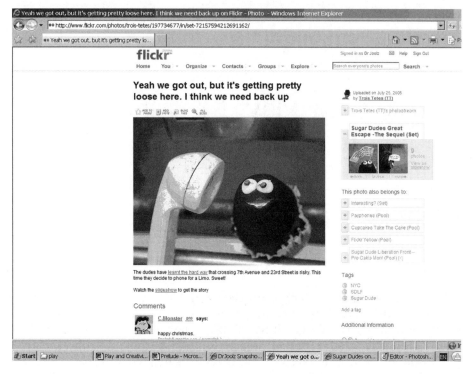

**Figure 2.1**  Sugardude on the 'phone (TroisTetes, 2006)

This incident illustrates a number of points; while all of us were involved in an activity that could undoubtedly be described as 'play', it was also one which could not have taken place without having acquired a range of complex social and literacy skills beforehand. Despite the absurdity of the activity, our play necessitated us drawing on, sharing and, arguably, developing aspects of our social and literacy skills. These included: organized teamwork; planning and preparation skills; understanding narrative structure; photographic techniques such as close-ups and establishing shots; and linguistic expertise to design titles, captions and tags to help tell the stories illustrated in the images. We had a strong sense that we wanted to draw in an audience who would enjoy the joke; wanting to make others laugh influenced the shots and the language we later used online. Our slideshows attracted many online comments, so the play moved continually across online and offline boundaries. Later, in Sweden, Ruminatrix took the play further and created her own story from cakes and home-made props (Ruminatrix, 2006). Thus, although she had not been in New York, Ruminatrix participated in parallel play elsewhere, extending the joke and demonstrating a cross-cultural inclusivity.

From the beginning, where we first saw C-Monster's images online, the fun depended on our ability to make connections with others through words and images. It is undoubtedly the case that without digital technology – our cameras and computers – we would neither have met, nor involved ourselves in this play. We would not have been able to create slideshows and we would not have been able to annotate our images in the way we did; certainly we would not have been able to present ourselves in such a way that we could discern common values and want to meet each other.

It is becoming increasingly clear that online social networking has become embedded in many people's offline lives across the world; while it is clear that many people learn the necessary skills to participate without tuition, there are implications for teachers in all this. I briefly indicate these implications here. First, I believe that social networking sites motivate learning. Secondly, the motivation to learn is partly triggered by the facility to collaborate and socialize with others. I believe that current classroom practices which focus mainly on individualized learning need to learn from what I and others (Gee, 2004; Williamson and Facer, 2004) have noted about online learning collaboration: that each individual can achieve more by interacting with others. Thirdly, I believe that social networking sites, with their structured formats and clear templates, are ideally suited to classroom learning, where students can look closely at the ways in which the written mode can interact with the visual and impact on meaning-making. Fourthly, with digital texts becoming increasingly multimodal, we now need to broaden our notion of what it means to be literate and include image production and analysis as part of normal procedure in the literacy classroom. Finally, with concerns being expressed about the dangers of online relationships (Byron, 2008), teachers have a role to play in introducing learners to critical reading skills.

This chapter is about digital text-making, online networking, play and learning. I show some of the ways in which people use a photo-sharing website (Flickr.com) not only to pursue leisure activities and to socialize, but as a space where they can collaborate and learn about digital text production and consumption, and about each other, the world and their place within it. I also suggest ways official education policy and practice might learn from such online social networking spaces as Flickr, not just in terms of students' literacy practices, but also in terms of looking beyond individual achievement and thinking about how to value collaborative group effort and achievement. In the next section I outline some of the theoretical frameworks I draw upon in thinking about play, new literacies and learning.

## New literacies and literacy as a social practice

Literacy is not just about decoding marks on a page; it is also about performing social acts of meaning, where meanings and practices vary according to context (Barton and Hamilton, 1998; Street, 1997). This definition is well illustrated by Web 2.0 spaces where individuals collaborate and socialize via online texts. Working from a functional linguistic theory of discourse (Halliday, 1985), theorists have described how the form a text takes is influenced by its social purpose and cultural context. Texts are therefore seen as being produced in response to, and out of, particular social situations, with text conceptualized as a social product and text-making as a social process. To put it at its most simple, effective communication depends upon choosing the right words (or other mode), to perform a particular task; different conventions are used to produce different text types, which perform different social tasks. Further, in terms of online networking, it is important to communicate in ways which 'fit' with different 'affinity spaces' (Gee, 2004): understanding the linguistic conventions, the ways in which one can present oneself and the features of the networking 'template' or site structure.

With a greater emphasis on context and literacy in practice, we can extend the notion of textuality. Further, in exploring meanings, we can take into account not just the written word, but also images, layout, font, sound, gesture, movement and so on. Acknowledging this broadened concept of textuality, literacy academics refer to multimodal texts (Kress and Van Leeuwen, 1996; 2001; Van Leeuwen and Jewitt, 2001) as well as 'digital literacies' (Davies, 2006a; Lankshear and Knobel, 2008). Technology has introduced new types of text, such as hypertext, and helped us to integrate a range of modes more easily, with multimodal online text production (for example, blogs, personal websites and social networking sites like MySpace.com) being taken up by thousands daily. Cashmore (2006), for example, cites MySpace as now having over 100 million accounts and Bebo as having 27 million, both of which are social networking sites mainly patronized by teenagers who use these online spaces to instant message, keep blogs, upload photographs, exchange music files, and much more. Lewis and Fabos, (2005) document how many young people feel they have been 'born into' technological practices, where their social lives are closely bound within their text production and consumption, and Carrington (2005, p. 13) writes of the 'new textual landscapes' into which 'children are being naturalised'.

## New literacies and old: domains of practice

Jewitt (2005) describes the enhanced role of images, particularly in screen-based texts where the visual is not just embellishment but plays a central semiotic role. Drawing on classroom research, she argues learners require guidance in reading multimodal texts and that we need to 'redefine the work of the reader' (Jewitt, 2005, p. 329). It has also been insistently argued that children's out-of-school practices need to be valued and developed in school, with Gee (2004), for example, vehement that 'children are having more and more learning experiences out of school that are more important for their futures than is much of the learning they do in school' (p. 5). In-school and out-of-school practices are clearly not mutually exclusive, and the work of Williams (2004), for example, shows how multi-ethnic children incorporate school discourses into their play, while Dowdall (2006) illustrates how a ten year old boy's home and school texts often blend, assimilating schooled and non-schooled practices. Yet the out-of-school literacy experiences described by many researchers (Beavis and Charles, 2005; Davies, 2006a; Gee, 2004; Merchant, 2004) take place through activities where participants' intentions are social, rather than academic. This is a key point to which I return.

Many new technologies provide routes to playful activities, that is, to recreational, experimental and informal pursuits. Assessment, learning aims and objectives set by non-participatory agents (for example, by government curricula or exam boards) are resoundingly absent, although counter-intuitively, clear aims and goals *are* frequently part of online play. The texts produced are often very rich, creative and even subversive. Online text making is an activity that can disrupt and interrogate traditional ways of doing things, such as using 'txt' message spellings and 'emoticons'; mixed fonts and cases; the creation and counter-intuitive valuing of very blurred or very boring images; videos of unusual topics; and sites with 'resistant' or irreverent messages (Davies, 2004; 2006a). They are spaces where critical literacy practices arise through creative play, and where 'preferred readings' are often undermined. Online practices are often exploratory, improvised, and bound up with people's social and cultural lives, seen by some as inappropriate for classroom settings (Lambirth, 2005). Lankshear and Knobel (2006) have pointed out that 'Learners' funds of knowledge very often have no place in the classroom and cannot have – since this would jeopardise professional expertise and challenge sectional interests that are served by schools' (p. 4).

Limitations of schooled conceptions of literacy both in the UK and elsewhere, as predominantly skills led and paper based, need to be expanded to systematically and consistently include digital texts, since these increasingly dominate in the wider sphere beyond classrooms, constituting the fabric of many people's social lives. As Honan (2008) finds, even where policy is more condoning of digital texts, barriers persist and prevent teachers using them habitually. The emphasis on a paper-based curriculum (policy *and* practice) means that dynamic, multilayered texts figure only marginally, and where technology is used, it is often applied in ways out of sync with out-of-school practices (Davies, 2006b). In talking of young people's out-of-school practices, Woolsey (2004) has argued that:

> these kids select from the range of technology options as an artist might from a palette, mixing and matching to accomplish their own goals; they don't focus on the technologies, but instead on the activities they want to engage and the goals that they might have set for themselves. They don't necessarily use the technologies in the ways they were intended, but instead tinker with them to accomplish things that please them. And they don't care much about the technologies in a technical or analytic sense, instead becoming immersed in the social environments that these technologies engender. (p. 1)

Further, it is often assumed that young learners *instinctively* know how to negotiate and read such text (Willett, in this volume). And it is true that many young people are very skilled; the blog of an eleven year old girl, Dylan (Verdi, 2005), whose video-blogging (vlogging) communicates effectively and widely, is a much cited case. The source of Dylan's expertise is clear; her father (Verdi, 2006) has guided and supported Dylan's work, but Dylan's friend (cited in Dylan's blog) has done less well and managed only one posting (Bria, 2005). Indeed, while the statistics for numbers of blogs are now astronomical at 35.3 million (Technorati, 2006), the cyberworld is littered with many blogs that have one or two posts and which are never sustained. Indeed, if we can talk about a 'digital divide', it resides *within*, as well as *across*, generations – a fact that those involved in education need to be wary of. While there are many young people involved in complex and sophisticated practices, there are many who are uninvolved, or who have problems in access and usage, and still others who could be offered further challenges to extend or reflect upon their experiences. Further, to think in terms of a single 'divide' is probably over simplistic, implying there are definite 'insiders' and 'outsiders', or as Prensky (2001) would have it 'digital natives and immigrants'. The picture is much more complex than this, and in this respect Byron (2008) draws out more subtle types of user.

The kinds of mediascape which digitally active young people inhabit out-of-school requires them to engage with multimodal texts, yet literacy classrooms tend to maintain a last-century emphasis on language. As Bober and Livingstone (2004) argue: 'children are in many ways confident of their new online skills … these should not be overestimated, for children are also aware of many ways in which they are confused, uncertain, or lacking in skills, thus resulting perhaps in a relatively narrow or problematically risky online experience' (p. 50). So, to pick up the point I made above, it is incumbent upon teachers and policy-makers to help structure the learning that many are participating in out-of-school literacy practices, so that we can value this out-of-school learning, provide further challenges and ensure universal access to these learning opportunities.

## Informal, collaborative, playful learning

While much important learning is happening outside the classroom, because it is built around social activities its aims remain social, and the learning informal, unplanned and stochastic. It is undoubtedly the informal, undirected, experimental dimension of this learning that makes it so compelling for many, and I am convinced by arguments (Gee, 2004; Morgan and Kennewell, 2005; Vygotsky, 1976) that playfulness can lead to productive outcomes in terms of learning and development. Huzinga (1949) has said that play is central to human culture, while Gee (2003) has argued that you have to break or customize the rules for learning to take place. Carter's (2004) work looking at creative language also reflects on how linguistic creativity is often born out of experimental, playful banter; something which Crystal endorses in his description of the ludic (Crystal, 1998). All communication is multimodal (Norris,

2004), so it is not surprising that play in one mode often triggers play in others; thus play with images, for example, often provokes playful, creative language.

While playfulness engenders learning, as Bober and Livingstone (2004) argue, play that occurs in some informal online activities may be narrowly focused, unchallenging and repetitive. Crucially, even for youngsters with technological access, their activities may be constrained by social goals as well as limitation in terms of their technology skills, or in their ability to see the possibilities available to them in different online spaces. For example, most young people's digital text-making tends to be directed to a specific, narrow social audience, such as within the friendship groups of those with whom they are already acquainted (Bortree, 2005; Boyd, 2006; Dowdall, 2006). Their 'diet' may therefore be restricted and repetitive, and they may simply need guidance, as indeed most do, when starting out in a new literacy domain. This is where schools can intervene, providing new challenges and direction, making learning less random, helping everyone to access digital texts, and to become self-aware, critical readers and producers of new literacies.

## Methodology

As I indicated in the opening of this chapter, I am a regular participant on Flickr and my observations derive strongly from my own experiences and understandings. Further, I have talked informally with groups of other so-called 'Flickrites' from London, Sheffield, Bristol and York in the UK, as well as with a group from New York. I have used email to carry out questionnaires and have used a blog (Phlickrblog.com) to ask others about their views and activities on Flickr. I have worked with teachers in schools on projects where Flickr has been used to develop critical literacy skills.

Lankshear and Knobel (2006) have drawn attention to the need for 'insider research': research focusing on those involved in new media *by* those who are also immersed in them. My involvement in Flickr allows me an insider perspective, but I have also been able to compare my experiences with others. In addition, I have looked closely across the site and used a multimodal approach (Kress and Van Leeuwen, 1996; 2001; Van Leeuwen and Jewitt, 2001) to consider the site 'as text', and to think about its affordances and constraints. I take into account words, images, textual layout, hyperlinks and other features in order to explore meanings. I reflect on how words and images are used by Flickr members in increasingly innovative ways, and how these practices reflect and facilitate the learning that is taking place online.

In this chapter I think about Flickr as a potential model for multimodal digital text-making, and learning through semi-structured activities. The examples I use instantiate learning opportunities which could be replicated in more formal educational situations. They are chosen to illustrate the potential of Flickr to develop visual awareness, multimodal text production and consumption, and social and Internet research skills. I argue that all these areas are part of literacy within subject English or as a cross-curricular strand, accepting the view that literacy is both social and multimodal.

## The Flickr website: organization of people and content

Flickr is a highly structured space, and members, as well as volunteer and salaried moderators, monitor activities on the site. It is free to join but there is more functionality, unlimited uploading and no visible ad-space for those who pay a nominal yearly charge. Members must be 13 years or over.

Flickr provides all members with an online space where they can manage their own 'photostream'; uploaded images are shown in chronological order and the template includes writing spaces for titles, descriptions and 'tags'. Tags are words or phrases that may define or label aspects of the image; they may be indexical, helping Flickr's search facility to locate the image. They may help the Flickrite catalogue their own images, through terms such as 'holiday', 'wedding', 'flowers' and so on. For example, anyone can search the Flickr tags and view others' 'holiday', 'wedding' or 'flower' images. Such a search provides much data for cross-cultural comparison of weddings and holidays for example. This is a highly valuable resource for teachers of all subjects and can provide much discussion material. Flickr members frequently subvert the nature of tags: for example, instead of giving one-word descriptors, they might write long phrases, obtuse remarks or quips. Titles can endorse or transform meanings of images of course, directing the gaze to particular features, or being suggestive of stories. An interesting exercise for a class is to provide titles for images and to see how meanings can change through this process. Descriptions can of course add more detail to the title, or can even undermine the meanings given.

Photographs can be arranged into sets on an individual's stream, and these sets can be grouped into broader 'collections'. These affordances promote thinking beyond individual photographs, extending the notion of text to narratives between images, and relationships across them, as well as providing a new way of looking at the world beyond. For example, for a set called 'literacy', photographers will gradually broaden their notion of what literacy entails. Looking at a series of images called 'literacy', provides a polysemic narrative about literacy and can promote discussion.

Members can initiate dialogue by commenting on and adding tags to others' images. 'Digital notes' can be superimposed on others' photographs, perhaps highlighting specific features, or suggesting how they may be cropped to achieve different effects. In school, teachers can invest in the fact that pupils already know each other and inhabit the same educational spaces, so that discussions might develop about representations of commonly known spaces, for example. Projects might include, like ones I have been involved in, students taking photographs of their school and their locality. In so doing, they learned about how the same spaces could be presented negatively or positively by using a range of angles, different lighting, or even varying from black and white to colour. Adding particular titles and verbal descriptions enhanced these effects. Pupils commented on each other's work, asked questions and learned how photographs do not simply represent reality, but that different approaches reflect different meanings.

## Communal groups

Any Flickr member can set up public groups to which anyone can contribute. Groups appear in a communal space, accessible via a number of on-site routes through hyperlinks. Images contributed by many photographers can be collected and viewed together in any kind of group. The instigator of a group, or 'admin', gives the group a title and provides a description or rubric of what is required for participation. Admins can remove 'unsuitable' images or even block particular members from participating. Reasons for blocking may include a history of being unfriendly or contributing 'inappropriate' or 'offensive' pictures; control is thus managed by members as well as by outside moderators if necessary. Many Flickr members collaborate most intensively in groups, since they not only pool their images in such spaces, but also open discussions about those images, the circumstances under which they were taken and how they fit (or not) the group's definitions. Interactivity is usually enthusiastic and lively, and jokes often develop. Some groups are specifically about teaching new skills and provide workshops on digital image manipulation, for example. Groups may comprise collections of images that feature specific colours, shapes, or perspectives, such as:

- 'The Red makes it';
- 'Beautiful Green';
- 'Squared circle';
- 'Looking down'; and
- 'Shooting up'.

Participation here raises visual awareness, and viewing these images together provides texts that show visual coherence. Some groups contain pictures which follow a particular tradition, for example,

- 'Martin Parr we ♥ U';
- 'Boring Postcards';
- 'Photograph like painting';
- 'Diane Arbus'; and
- 'Name that Film'.

Here, members demonstrate their understanding of a particular genre or style and build on previous knowledge. Viewing these images collectively enhances such knowledge and provides a particular perspective on many aspects of our world. Other groups focus on finding particular patterns such as repeated designs or marks, interesting prints or textures, reflections or symmetrical designs, and so on. Many groups use the internet as a kind of virtual gallery for street art, or 'graffiti', with groups like:

- 'Walls Speak to us';
- 'Girls on Walls';
- 'Visual Resistance';
- 'Stencils';
- 'Banksy'; and
- 'Wet shame graffiti'.

Such groups provide a new context for showing street art, bringing it a new lease of life in a new exhibition space and allowing it to be seen as part of a socio-political movement rather than vandalism. Such groups, for example, provide potential discussion material, perhaps about social issues and politics, or maybe around images of street art and debating whether it is a democratic art form or urban crime.

There are groups that draw on games whose roots reach back to other traditions; groups such as:

- 'Visual Bingo';
- 'Snap'; and
- 'Picture Dominoes'.

Such groups develop and require teamwork, collaboration and close observation skills for participation. Other groups have an interest in narrative, for example the '5 picture story' group requires individuals to upload five images which tell a story; 'photo dominoes' requires members to contribute an image which relates in some way to the previous one, thematically or content-wise; 'domestic spaces – human spaces' requires images of items in domestic spaces that leave a clue of what has happened before, and so on.

Some group admins monitor members' contributions to their group pools of images very closely, even removing those that do not fit the rubric they have set out. Members are therefore required to choose their shots carefully, and will sometimes go to great lengths, giving elaborate linguistic descriptions with their shots, to justify the inclusion of their images in the group pool. In terms of learning, participants start to understand how the framing of a particular image may give it a slightly different nuance; how perhaps the manipulation of colour (maybe through lighting, type of film, or even through the use of software such as Photoshop) can affect the meaning of an image.

Some groups are immensely successful, having many members, thousands of images and lively discussion threads. Other groups have sparse numbers of images. It is clear that there are things to be learned about the set-up and maintenance of groups. Groups are an excellent way of structuring activities and, while allowing a whole range of creative responses, provide rules for participation and learning.

Teachers can set up groups for pupils so that they can contribute images. They can be involved in thinking about titling images, tagging them, offering pithy descriptions and commenting on others' photographs. Such activities allow students to write within templates and to think carefully about their use of language to highlight particular aspects of the visual text. English teachers might want to ask classes to take images that illustrate metaphors of their own making, or they may ask pupils to take images that illustrate aspects of a poem or play. Drama teachers might ask pupils to take images that represent moments in a play. Some uses of Flickr allow pupils to think in detail about the relationship between the visual and the linguistic. Across the curriculum there will be other kinds of use, such as images of the locality used in geography. For photography classes, the possibilities for encouraging peer review of each others' work is immense.

## Safety issues

The default setting is that images are visible to anyone who belongs to Flickr. However, one can alter this default and make images available only for specific audiences; in school terms this may mean restricted access to pupils in a class and possibly their parents. Under each image there is space for the 'owner' to write a description and then a further (potentially endless) space for comments to be left. Commenters must be members of Flickr, and it is impossible to leave anonymous remarks. Owners of a photostream can delete comments from photos and can block particular people from being able to see or comment on their images. Witnessing pupils using Flickr in the classroom allowed me to see how pupils quickly learned that comments left on images need to be carefully written, that tact and diplomacy needs to be learned, and that witty remarks are highly valued and skilled ways of using language. In terms of teaching pupils about skills for social networking online, it was invaluable for pupils to immediately see how their remarks were being received. Because pupils were in the classroom while they wrote online, they could immediately see each others' reactions to their remarks and this was of benefit. As Brooks (2005) explains:

> The thing I like about getting images from Flickr is the students can see that there are real people behind the images, not some generic, faceless website. Real people, like them, have created the pictures, shared them with everyone else, and usually only asked to be credited. There are all kinds of lessons to be taught in those actions.

This is a powerful notion since learners can see that they have something to offer others; there are learners and teachers, but these roles are not formally designated and vary as activities change.

## Conclusions

As Gee (2004) has argued, traditional schooling is based on individual isolated activities that are individually assessed. Collaborative learning has a great deal to offer in terms of learning but also in terms of its relevance to the ways in which people tend to operate in out-of-school domains.

On Flickr, the creation of content (images and written text), and sharing it online through social interaction, brings social constructivist explanations for learning to the fore (Vygotsky, 1978; Wenger 1998), since individuals bring their own ideas and contributions, and can then interact over these. Interactions frequently bring new perspectives to interpretation or development of the content. The shared endeavour of image-making means that because individuals are all in the same position of wanting to create powerful texts, power is distributed and comments tend to be constructive, supportive and enthusiastic.

I have previously argued that, on Flickr, the nature of the learning is concerned with multimodal literacy development as well as developing social and cultural awareness (Davies, 2006a). I have also argued that the learning that takes place on Flickr is informal 'social learning' (Lave and Wenger, 1991; Wenger, 1998); the learning takes place through the execution of particular activities that are collaboratively developed and have aims and objectives other than learning. I have described how Flickr fosters ways of learning, 'where individuals ... reconsider the way they see themselves and their social worlds. ... where new sets of social practices and codes of conduct evolve over time, allowing individuals to re-examine some of their experiences whilst acquiring new ones' (Davies, 2006a, p. 218). In this chapter I have shown the potential for play and learning on Flickr, and described how it provides structures for individual and group participation which can be safely adopted in school.

## References

Barton, D. and Hamilton, M. (1998) *Local Literacies: Reading and Writing in One Community*. London: Routledge.

Beavis, C. and Charles, C. (2005) 'Challenging notions of gendered game play: teenagers playing "The Sims"', *Discourse: Studies in the Cultural Politics of Education*, 26(3): 355–68.

Bober, M. and Livingstone, S. (2004) *UK Children Go Online: Listening to Young People's Experiences*. London: Media@LSE.

Bortree, D.S. (2005) 'Presentation of self on the Web: an ethnographic study of teenage girls' "weblogs"', *Education, Communication and Information*, 5: 25–39.

Boyd, D. (2006) 'G/localization: When global information and local interaction collide', paper presented at the Emerging Technology Conference, March, San Diego, California. Retrieved 1 August 2006, from www.danah.org/papers/Etech2006.html

Bria. (2005) *It's My World*. Retrieved 2 February 2005, from www.brianadine.blogspot.com/

Brooks, S. (2005) *Flickr Creative Commons*. Retrieved 10 October 2005, from www.edugadget.com/2005/05/07/flickr-creative-commons/

Byron, T. (2008) *Safer Children in a Digital World: The Report of the Byron Review*. London: DCSF Publications. Retrieved 3 May 2008, from: www.dfes.gov.uk/byronreview/pdfs/Final%20Report%20Bookmarked.pdf

C-Monster (2004) *Sugardudes: The Set*. Retrieved 4 July 2006, from www.flickr.com/photos/arte/sets/112574/

Carrington, V. (2005) 'New textual landscapes, information and early literacy', in J. Marsh (ed.), *Popular Culture, New Media and Digital Literacy in Early Childhood*. London: RoutledgeFalmer. pp. 13–27.

Carter, R. (2004) *Language and Creativity; The Art of Common Talk*. London: Routledge.

Cashmore, P. (2006) *Mashable! Social networking 2.0*. Retrieved 17 November 2006, from http://mashable.com

Crystal, D. (1998) *Language Play*. London: Penguin.

Davies, J. (2004) 'Negotiating femininities on-line', *Gender and Education*, 16(1): 35–49.

Davies, J. (2006a) 'Affinities and beyond! Developing ways of seeing in online spaces', *E-learning*, 3(2): 217–34.

Davies, J. (2006b) 'Nomads and tribes: online meaning-making and the development of new literacies', in J. Marsh and E. Millard (eds), *Popular Literacies and Schooling*. London: Routledge. pp. 161–76.

Dowdall, C. (2006) 'Ben and his army scenes: a consideration of one child's out-of-school text production', *English in Education*, 40(3): 39–54.

Gee, J.P. (2003) *What Video Games Have to Teach Us About Learning and Literacy*. New York: Palgrave Macmillan.

Gee, J.P. (2004) *Situated Language and Learning: A Critique of Traditional Schooling*. London: Routledge.

Halliday, M.A.K. (1985) *An Introduction to Functional Grammar*. London: Edward Arnold.

Honan,E. (2008) 'Barriers to teachers using digital texts in literacy classrooms', *Literacy*, 42(1): 36–43.

Huzinga, J. (1949) *Homo Ludens: A Study of the Play Element in Culture*. New York and London: Routledge.

Jewitt, C. (2005) 'Multimodality, "Reading" and "Writing" for the 21st Century', *Discourse*, 26(3): 315–31.

Kress, G. and Van Leeuwen, T. (1996) *Reading Images: The Grammar of Visual Design*. London: Routledge.

Kress, G. and Van Leeuwen, T. (2001) *Multimodal Discourse: The Modes and Media of Contemporary Communication*. Oxford: Edward Arnold.

Lambirth, A. (2005) 'Don't they get enough of that at home?', *Literacy*, 39(2): 97–103.

Lankshear, C. and Knobel, M. (2006) *New Literacies 2.0: Everyday Practices and Classroom Learning*. Buckingham: Open University Press.

Lankshear, C. and Knobel, M. (2008) *Digital Literacies: Concepts, Policies and Practices*. New York: Peter Lang.

Lave, J. and Wenger, E. (1991) *Situated Learning*. Cambridge: Cambridge University Press.

Lewis, C. and Fabos, B. (2005) 'Instant messaging, literacies and social identities', *Reading Research Quarterly*, 40(4): 470–501.

Merchant, G. (2004) 'Imagine all that stuff really happening: narrative and identity in children's on-screen writing', *E-learning*, 3(1): 341–57.

Morgan, A. and Kennewell, S. (2005) 'The role of play in the pedagogy of ICT', *Education and Information Technologies*, 10(3): 177–88.

Norris, S. (2004) *Analyzing Multimodal Interaction: A Methodological Framework*. London: Routledge.

Prensky, M. (2001) 'Digital natives, digital immigrants', *On the Horizon*, 9(5), October. Retrieved 22 August 2008, from: www.twitchspeed.com/site/Prensky%20-%20Digital%20Natives,%20Digital%20Immigrants%20-%20Part1.htm

Ruminatrix. (2006) *sockergubbarna befrielsefront*. Retrieved 6 October 2006, from www.flickr.com/photos/ruminatrix/sets/72057594127030623/

Street, B. (1997) 'The implications of the new literacy studies for education', *English in Education*, 31(3): 45–59.

Technorati (2006) *State of the Blogosphere, April 2006. Part 1: On Blogosphere Growth*. Retrieved 16 October 2006, from http://technorati.com/weblog/2006/04/96.html

TroisTetes (2005) *Comment on 'Sugardudes' Image*. Retrieved 6 October 2005, from: www.flickr.com/photos/arte/4424203/in/set-112574#comment1994029

TroisTetes (2006) *Yeah We Got Out, but It's Getting Pretty Loose Here. I Think We Need Back Up*. Retrieved 6 October 2006, from www.flickr.com/photos/trois-tetes/197734677/in/set-72157594212691162/

Van Leeuwen, T. and Jewitt, C. (2001) *The Handbook of Visual Analysis*. London: Sage.

Verdi, D. (2005) *The Dylan Show*. Retrieved 16 October, 2006, from: http://dylanverdi.com/index.php/2005/01/02/the-whole-story/.

Verdi, M. (2006) *Secrets of Videoblogging*. Berkeley, CA: Peachpit Press.

Vygotsky, L.S. (1976) 'Play and its role in the mental development of the child', in J.S. Bruner, A. Jolly and K. Sylva (eds), *Play: Its Role in Development and Evolution*. London: Penguin. pp. 537–54. (Reprinted from *Soviet Psychology*, 1967, 5(3): 6–18.)

Vygotsky, L.S. (1978) *Thought and Language*. Cambridge, MA: Harvard University Press.

Wenger, E. (1998) *Communities of Practice*. Cambridge: Cambridge University Press.

Williams, A. (2004) '"Right, get your book bags!"' Siblings playing school in multiethnic London', in E. Gregory, S. Long and D. Volk (eds), *Many Pathways to Literacy*. London: RoutledgeFalmer. pp. 52–65.

Williamson, B. and Facer, K. (2004) 'More than just a game: the implications for schools of children's computer game communities', *Education, Communication and Information*, 4(2/3), 255–70.

Woolsey, K. (2004) *Digital Kids and Media: An Overview and 4 Digital Questions*. Retrieved 1 September 2006, from www.exploratorium.edu/research/digitalkids/Woolsey_DigitalKids

# Download

## Key points

1. Digital texts are frequently multimodal and thus readers need to be aware of how images can represent 'reality' in different ways. Teachers need to help learners become critical readers of multimodal texts.
2. Online spaces are set up in ways that facilitate interactivity over text-making. The structures used by many online spaces can also be utilized in classrooms to channel interactivity in particular ways and to structure learning.
3. Teachers can build on young people's existing interests in social uses of technology and take them further in their learning.

## In your classroom

1. Encourage students to invent titles for images selected by the teacher from Flickr. Discussion on how titles and tags can change the meanings of images. Students can take photographs and share these either via a photo-sharing site like Flickr, or through other digital means. Students can similarly suggest alternative titles and descriptive paragraphs which alter the way the images are read.
2. Students take digital images of the locality and experiment with angle, colour, lighting and crops to alter the way the images present the environment. Discussion about the use of images as documenting reality and how they can present a range of meanings, especially when accompanied by text.
3. Students contribute to groups of images set up in relation to a project. The images are used as a bank of resources which reflect different aspects of a project, and which show different ways of exploring an issue.

## Further reading

Burnett. R. (2005) *How Images Think*. Cambridge, MA: The MIT Press.
Davies, J. and Merchant, G. (2008) *Web 2.0 for Schools: Social Participation and Learning*. New York: Peter Lang.
Richardson, W. (2006) *Blogs, Wikis, Podcasts and Other Powerful Web Tools for Classrooms*. Thousand Oaks, CA: Corwin Press.

# 3

# Masters and Critics: Children as Producers of Online Digital Texts

*Clare Dowdall*

## Introduction

With the introduction and phenomenal growth of popular social network sites such as Bebo, MySpace and Facebook,[i] increasing numbers of school-age children are regularly producing digital texts as by-products of online social networking (Childnet International, 2007a ; Ofcom, 2008). The digital texts that children create can exist across widely and locally distributed networks of friends and acquaintances. They are often designed to showcase the owner of the text and share information with a selected audience. Digital texts can vary tremendously from the print- and paper-based texts that school-age children are required to produce as part of the English curriculum (Department for Education and Employment/Qualifications and Curriculum Authority, 1999). Arguably, the masteries involved to successfully create these different types of texts may vary. This chapter explores the *profile pages* that children create in online social network sites. These are digital texts where still and moving images, words, sound and graphics are combined to create a representation of the owner for members within their online social network to view and communicate with. The creation of a profile page depends on the rapidly evolving affordances of the digital media involved. These texts are often multimodal (Bearne, 2003; Pahl and Rowsell, 2005), including, in addition to words, uploaded photographs, videos, music and feedback comments from other people. These profiles can be viewed and used as artefacts of multimodal communication and identity. As such they are highly purposeful, powerful and of consequence to the creator.

A rapidly growing body of research is concerned with the new textual and communicative possibilities offered by the digital literacies that children are able to access (Boyd, 2007; Boyd and Ellison, 2007; Carrington, 2005; Davies, 2007; Marsh, 2005, Marsh et al., 2005). This field has been emerging since the World Wide Web has been reconceptualized in Web 2.0 terms as a social and creative platform for communication. Within this field, concepts of literacy, text and communication are melding to such an extent that the act of text production can be viewed as a by-product of social networking, where the act of creating a text is driven as much by a social and technological mastery as the ability to be functionally literate (Dowdall, 2006). Liu (2007), who has examined the use of over 127,000 MySpace profile pages, emphasizes the social forces propelling children's online text production in these contexts. He argues that social network sites provide forums where everyday tastes can be moulded and performed for an audience. Drawing upon Goffman's (1959) concept of everyday performance, Liu (2007) describes these sites as 'one of the newest stages for online textual performance of self'.

Based on the growing body of research in this field, it is clear that children's text production is evolving alongside new technologies and accompanying social activities. This notion is exciting for researchers and educators. However, in England, since the introduction of specific national strategies designed to improve literacy standards (Department for Education and Employment, 1998; Department for Education and Skills, 2006), children's mastery as text producers using established forms of print-based text has remained the major educational and political concern. The creation of a child's profile page can be viewed as a form of text production that occurs beyond these institutions, and that differs from curriculum-directed text production. This difference is the source of tension for some parents, educators and policy-makers as children seize ownership of the text-producing process in contexts that are inaccessible to the institutions that conventionally assume responsibility for it. This chapter aims to explore this tension using examples from children's profile pages.

The screenshot in Figure 3.1 is taken from a fourteen-year-old girl, Clare's, MySpace profile. It is included here to orientate readers who may not be familiar with social network profile pages. Clare is a subject of my doctoral research and has given permission for this screenshot to be included here. I am currently included as a member of Clare's online social network as one of her *friends*. Clare has set her profile to a private setting. This means that only the people who she invites to join her network, by email, as friends can see the information that is displayed. Clare has had her MySpace profile since June 2006. She regularly changes the appearance of her profile page by changing her user name and replacing the featured photographs, music and *about me* blurb. Currently on her MySpace profile page, Clare includes two images of herself: a recent photograph from a skiing holiday, and a party shot, taken with friends. Clare is currently using the user name *Clarei* and has uploaded music for her friends to play. A brief *about me* section provides Clare with the opportunity to describe herself in her own words. There are opportunities for friends who have access to Clare's site to post comments in response to her *pics* and *videos,* and there is a messaging service for friends to contact Clare directly and privately.

**Figure 3.1**  Clare's MySpace profile, February 2008

The creation of this profile occurs as part of Clare's daily recreational activities, and varies in many ways from the directed text production that she engages with during the school day. One key difference that has been observed is that new technologies allow children unprecedented power and authority as publishers and disseminators of text (Bearne, 2005; Kress, 2003). This power partly resides in the opportunities that children now have to generate and publish texts to widespread audiences in online spaces. In addition, this power is fuelled by the ability of children to exclude the traditional safeguarding forces in society from their online activities. For example, Clare employs the privacy options currently offered by MySpace to prevent unsolicited viewing of her profile pages. However, while this assures Clare's privacy and safety from unwanted attention online, Clare's parents and teachers are also denied the opportunity to oversee her online digital footprint.[ii] Consequently, as Clare produces texts beyond the surveillance of family and school, the opportunities for safeguarding and protecting Clare from the consequences of her texts can be perceived as being diminished by these institutions.

The notion that it is increasingly hard, yet necessary, to safeguard children in online contexts is occuring at a time in England when high-stakes testing in schools, and the enhancement of parental accountability, remain high-profile political issues. The recently published *Children's Plan* (Department for Children, Schools, and Families, 2007) claims in its foreword that parents want and need more support to raise their children safely in British society.[iii] Equally, the foreword to *The Byron Review* (DCSF, 2008) highlights the perceived risks associated with children's use of new technology, and the sense of panic experienced by parents and caregivers who do not fully engage with new technologies.[iv] Surrounding the reported sense of parental concern identified in these influential reports is a widespread media discourse about the perceived threat to children from online predators in social network sites (*BBC Panorama: One Click from Danger*, 2007). This media discourse contributes to the tension that is created as surveillance of children's text production in online contexts becomes more problematic in a society that is calling for parents to take increasing responsibility for their children's safety and behaviour. In relation to text production, therefore, children can be viewed as having the potential to be increasingly powerful agents in digital landscapes, while parents and educational institutions are less able to exert authority and control. Accordingly, the discourse surrounding this situation constructs children as text producers from a deficit rather than asset perspective.

While children's safety in online spaces will always be of paramount concern to parents and educators, I would like to suggest that a more positive view of children's digital text production could be aspired to. The theoretical frameworks offered by various critical literacy proponents (Freebody and Luke, 1990; Freire and Macedo, 1987) provide a mechanism for viewing children's text production in online spaces that challenge the protectionist discourse that surrounds children's use of social network sites. From various critical literacy perspectives, texts and their creation and consumption in any context – digital or not – can be viewed as a political and social endeavour. Effective critical literacy involves the interrogation of texts in relation to the social and cultural contexts in which they are produced. Freire, through teaching critical literacy, saw the development of active questioning of social reality as the route to empowerment for unempowered Brazilian workers in the 1960s (Gee, 1996, pp. 37–8). An evolved and more widely applied interpretation of critical literacy is offered by Luke and Carrington (2002, p. 245) who 'argue for a kind of critical literacy that envisions literacy as a tool for remediating one's relation to the global flows of capital and information, bodies and images'. Both of these interpretations recognize that critical literacy holds transformative potential for the individuals who are involved in interacting with texts that can never be politically or socially neutral. This notion is illustrated in the Four Resources Model of Reading (Freebody and Luke, 1990). This model requires that interaction with texts (reading and writing) involves not only code-breaking and meaning-making at word and text level, but that a pragmatic and critical competence are necessary too (Luke and Freebody, 1999). Here, Luke and Freebody detail how the seeming neutrality of texts needs to be challenged for the underlying ideologies, and for the economic and cultural influences that play upon them, in order that the reader/writer can become effectively literate within their local and global communities.

It would seem that a critical literacy approach that emphasizes unpicking, exploring and transforming the power relations housed within and around texts, as well as an interrogation of the interplaying economic and cultural forces that act upon texts, is a necessary component of children's text production in digital contexts. This chapter attempts to explore children's digital text production from a critical literacy perspective. By identifying the masteries that are involved in being a successful and critical producer of online digital texts, I will attempt to develop a concept of *critical digital literacy to use alongside children's online text production.* It is hoped that by considering children's online profile pages in this way, their online text production can be framed positively, with an emphasis on the creative, critical and skilful approach that they take as they produce texts to fulfil a range of functions.

## Children of the strategies

Young teenagers in England who are currently involved in online social networking are also the sector of the population that has been educated under New Labour's education policies. In 1997, the incoming Labour government described education as their top priority.[v] Building from the pilot study introduced during the Conservative government's final year in office, the Labour Party has been responsible for the introduction of the *National Literacy Strategy Framework for Teaching* (DfEE, 1998) and the *Primary National Strategy* (DfES, 2006), in an attempt to raise the standards of literacy within England and Wales. Two children are described in this chapter: Clare and Tom. In 1998, just as the *National Literacy Strategy Framework for Teaching* (DfEE, 1998) was introduced, Clare and Tom were beginning their formal education in primary school. Consequently, I have labelled Clare and Tom as *children of the strategies,* as both children have been educated for their entire primary education by teachers using the national strategies. Beyond school however, Clare and Tom are both keen and regular users of the social network sites Bebo and MySpace. They have both been selected and interviewed as participants in my doctoral research based on their enthusiastic use of social network sites. This research aims to understand how digital texts are used by a small purposive sample of pre-teenage and early teenage children to create and perform their social identities. Data drawn from semi-structured interviews and discussion about the digital texts that Clare and Tom have created forms the basis for the arguments included in this chapter.

## Clare

Clare is fourteen years old and in Year ten at state secondary school. She is currently in the first year of public examination coursework (GCSE). In English studies, she is reading and learning about the play *An Inspector Calls*. According to Clare, this involves writing essays by hand for her tutor, or perhaps an examiner, she is unsure which. She explains that coursework is not allowed to be written and submitted using a computer in case she cheats or her tutor alters it. At home Clare has her own laptop computer with broadband internet access, which she uses every day for communicating with her friends. Currently she has an active MySpace account and a neglected Bebo account. Both these accounts are private and can only be viewed by members of Clare's online social network. Clare is a sophisticated and experienced user of social network sites. She created her first Bebo quiz in April 2005, followed by her first MySpace profile page in June 2006. She has been an avid communicator using MSN instant messenger, Bebo and MySpace since then. Although Clare created her Bebo account first, she now feels that MySpace is a more appropriate social network site to use, with Bebo being 'too simple' and 'for chavs'. Clare's evaluation of Bebo and MySpace reflects how she perceives them as useful accoutrements to her creation of image and identity. The texts that she creates can be viewed as artefacts of Clare's desired social identities (Pahl, 2007; Pahl and Rowsell, 2005): sites where Clare realizes a material presence through the multimodal text production process. Clare views this process as critically as another image-conscious teenager might view the purchase of a new pair of sports shoes. For Clare, the act of text production using social network sites is a significant social and recreational activity, which she engages with in order to create a desired impression of herself to her peers.

## Tom

Tom is thirteen years old and in Year nine at state secondary school. In English lessons Tom describes how he is 'doing Shakespeare'. According to Tom, this involves participating in a range of activities including completing character quizzes and watching film versions of Shakespeare's plays. In terms of text production, Tom recalls having to write long answers by hand to questions set by his teacher. Recently he has been using a school laptop to search for poems and write about them. These texts have been printed out and submitted to his teacher for marking. At home, Tom has access to the family computer, which is in the office room. He uses this on a daily basis, following negotiations with his parents, to stay in touch with his friends. Tom has a personal Bebo account, and a personal MySpace account, both of which are private accounts visible only to contacts within his social network. He also has a shared open-access MySpace account which he created with his friend, Sam, to showcase their band's music. Tom began using social network sites and MSN instant messenger in 2006. At school, Tom is already recognized as

*Continued*

*Continued*

a talented musician. His uncle is a professional musician, and has his own MySpace account. It seems reasonable to suggest that Tom's uncle has influenced the creation of Tom's shared MySpace account, and has contributed to the way that Tom views social network sites as tools that fulfil different practical and recreational functions, such as keeping in touch with friends and publicizing his music.

According to Clare and Tom, their everyday use of social network sites is typical within their peer groups. This anecdotal claim about the endemic reach of online social networking is supported generally by a wide range of data sources and media reporting (Office of Communications, 2008). Access to the internet from home continues to grow rapidly. The National Statistics Office currently states that 61 per cent of British households now have internet access, a growth of 36 per cent since 2002 (National Statistics, 2008). Alongside this statistic, the use of online social network sites is reported as being extremely popular: the *Communications Market Reports 2007* (Office of Communications, 2007) reveals that the social network sites Bebo, MySpace, Facebook and YouTube are in the top 10 websites by time spent online. Alexa, the web ranking company, reports that MySpace and Bebo are the ninth and tenth most visited websites in the UK (Alexa, 2008). These claims are supported by media and online sources that repeatedly report how social network sites have seen phenomenal growth. According to Wikipedia,[vi] MySpace is currently reported as having 217 million accounts and Bebo 40 million accounts. While these data are not verified, the tremendous amount of media, government and research attention recently given to children's online activities demonstrates the widespread interest in online social networking in the lives of UK adults and children today (BBC *Panorama*, 2007; Childnet International, 2007a; DCFS, 2008; Livingstone and Bober, 2005; Livingstone and Haddon, 2007).

## Children and their literacy

The rapid growth of online social networking as a recreational activity has affected Clare and Tom as they have learnt to produce texts in online social networks. Equally, during the 10-year period of Clare and Tom's formal education, the art and skill of composing and presenting classroom texts has been made a top educational priority. Numerous research projects have been funded and resources have been provided to support educators as they endeavour to raise children's abilities in writing, as measured by statutory national testing (Office for Standards in Education, 2003; United Kingdom Literacy Association/ Primary National Strategy, 2004; Younger and Warrington, 2005). Clare and Tom's formal education has been driven by a strong focus on developing functional and skills-based literacy as a result of current high-stakes assessment regimes and teacher accountability (Grainger, 2004). Street (1993) describes this type of institutionally driven skills-based literacy as 'autonomous literacy'; a view which recognizes literacy as 'a separate, thing-like object which people should acquire as a set of decontextualised skills' (Pahl and Rowsell, 2005, p. 14). Clare and Tom have both achieved acceptable standards of 'literacy' according to their national test scores for writing. By achieving the desired level in their Key Stage 2 writing tests, they have both demonstrated (according to the parameters imposed by the test and mark scheme), for their teachers, parents and policy-makers, that they have mastered the skill of writing. In educational and skills-based terms, they are literate children who have succeeded during and despite the implementation of various strategies to enhance children's schooled and tested literacy attainment.

## Children and their digital literacy

It is clear from these limited descriptions that as well as being *children of the strategies*, Clare and Tom are also motivated producers and consumers of digital texts in and around online settings. Equally therefore, Clare and Tom can be described as *children of the new digital age* (Marsh, 2005); children who, as long as they can remember, have been surrounded by ever-evolving digital technologies and practices that impact on their daily existence, and the textual landscapes that they occupy (Carrington, 2005). Accordingly, they have developed the capacity to be literate in this digital textual landscape, as well as within their educational settings. Therefore, in addition to their measured educational literacy, Clare and Tom can also be regarded as children who are digitally literate.

The European Commission has recently attempted to define digital literacy through the DigEuLit project. The first project report offers the following definition:

> Digital Literacy is the awareness, attitude and ability of individuals to appropriately use digital tools and facilities to identify, access, manage, integrate, evaluate, analyse and synthesize digital resources, construct new knowledge, create media expressions, and communicate with others, in the context of specific life situations, in order to enable constructive social action; and to reflect upon this process. (Martin, 2006)

This definition emphasizes that digital literacy involves competence around tools and facilities within specific contexts, and reflects the view held by Dobson and Willinsky (in press): that digital literacy, while being a contested term, can be defined simply as reading and writing using letters, numbers, images and sound that have been conveyed electronically. Along with skills-based definitions of literacy, these definitions of digital literacy are also restricted to the functional. However, catalysed by the early work of the New London Group (1996), definitions of literacy and text have continued to expand and fragment in relation to evolving textual forms. In and around school, new digital textual possibilities mean that teachers and students increasingly recognize that text production can be a multimodal endeavour, where words, images, music and sound can combine to create rich texts that are driven by a desire to communicate powerfully and appropriately within a given medium. In addition to recent changes to the National Literacy Strategy framework guidance (Department for Education and Skills, 2006) the Qualifications and Curriculum Authority (QCA) have published two key texts, *More than Words: Multimodal Texts in the Classroom* (QCA, 2004) and *More than Words 2: Creating Stories on Page and Screen* (QCA, 2005), to enhance teachers' awareness of expanding notions of text, and the multimodal communication that is facilitated by the digital technologies that are increasingly available in schools and homes throughout the UK. In these documents, the importance of the role of the screen as a portal for housing children's texts is championed, in an attempt to support teachers as they respond to teaching the broad demands of screen-based text production. However, the emphasis on new screen-based textual forms and associated text production in digital contexts, which is promoted by the new Primary National Strategy for literacy (DFES, 2006) and QCA documents (QCA, 2004; 2005), only partly reflects how definitions of literacy have expanded. While these documents endeavour to promote the digital literacies that are afforded by new technologies, they do not take full account of the New Literacies Studies paradigm (Marsh, 2005) of which digital literacy is now an established part.

## Children and their critical digital literacy

When considered from a New Literacies Studies perspective (Barton and Hamilton, 2000; New London Group, 1996), the term 'digital literacy' invokes a sociocultural definition of literacy that brings to the fore the socially situated qualities of any discourse situation (Pahl, 2007). From this perspective, literacy (specifically here, the act of creating an online profile page) is viewed as far more than the production of a multimodal text using new digital technologies. Instead, the New Literacy Studies paradigm requires us to regard acts of text creation as socially motivated behaviour, enacted as part of a large 'D' Discourse, where 'language-in-use' and the 'other stuff' of communication (gesture, symbols, attitudes, experiences) combine to allow meaningful communication within a context (Gee, 1996, p. 7). Viewing children's online profile page production from within the New Literacy Studies paradigm enables skills-based autonomous definitions of digital literacy to be subsumed into much broader definitions of literacy and multiliteracies, which begin from the premise that children create texts, digital or otherwise, as part of their wider social practices. In order to succeed socially, as well as academically, across the myriad opportunities for text production available in the early twenty-first century, children must possess the ability to interrogate and recognize the power relations and forces that play upon and around their text production. This ability can be described as the possession of critical digital literacy: a mastery of the wider sociocultural and economic context in which text production in digital spaces occurs.

From a critical digital literacy perspective, the creation of a profile page is clearly socially motivated behaviour, where the power relations that exist around the text are explored, unpicked and possibly transformed. Clare's profile page, where photographs, music and 'about me' statements converge digitally to form a dynamic screen-based text, vividly illustrates how digital texts can be viewed as more than the product of technical skill. Clare's attitudes and experiences are inscribed into this text, and projected from it, as she uses it to position herself among her audience. This text has meaning and purpose for Clare that transcends performing her technical skill in screen-based contexts. For Clare, this text can be seen as a vehicle for negotiating her desired social identities (Gee, 1996, p. 91); an informal space for her to participate in a social network that is circumscribed by the affordances of the technologies, and the social and cultural practices and resources available to group members. These networks can be described as communities of practice (Wenger, 1998) or affinity groups (Gee, 2003, p. 27): sites where the behaviour and masteries of the group's insiders are recognizable to others within the same semiotic domain. This attention to the local and wider context in which a text is created reflects Clare's ability as a critically digitally literate text producer. By focusing on the context for communication, Clare recognizes that any text produced becomes a by-product and an artefact of social negotiation and positioning, as well as a reflection of her technical ability with the tools and media being used.

Based on the discussion so far, Clare and Tom can be regarded as doubly literate: they are literate in relation to autonomous skills-based views of literacy (Street, 1993) and digital literacy, as well as literate in relation to a wider New Literacies Studies interpretation of the term. I am not intending to imply here that these literacies and contexts are exclusive. For those charged with the responsibility of teaching children like Clare and Tom, the converging and interweaving nature of these textual landscapes needs to be recognized as children move fluidly from classroom to playground and home, engaging in a wide variety of textual practices.

Clearly, these landscapes unite fluidly around Clare and Tom. For them, the switch from one text-producing context to the next is just a normal part of what it means to exist in a twenty-first-century multiliteracies landscape (New London Group, 1996). Being able to succeed as text producers in academic institutions and online contexts indicates that Clare and Tom are learning the rules of producing texts in these different contexts, and have mastered the ability to switch effortlessly from one form of text production to another. Part of this mastery involves possessing a sense of criticality born from the ability to position yourself in relation to others through the textual artefacts that you create. As well as demonstrating a social mastery in relation to their local networks, Clare and Tom demonstrate that they can read the wider context in which they produce their texts for different purposes and audiences. This aspect of critical digital literacy can be viewed as a quality that transcends and connects context and genre. In short, successful communicators at school as

well as in online networks are able to demonstrate the full range of competences proposed by Freebody and Luke (1990) in the Four Resources Model of
Reading, within and around a range of local and global contexts unimaginable
even twenty years ago.

## Critical digital literacy: building an asset perspective

To explore how children's profile page creation can demonstrate evidence of
critical digital literacy, I include here some descriptions based on a recent
interview with Tom and his friend Sam. Tom and Sam are both thirteen. They
were introduced to MySpace and Bebo at friends' and cousins' houses. For
these boys, the sociable act of creating and consuming texts together around
a computer is as much a part of the process of online social networking as
publishing texts for an online audience. Tom and Sam have together created
an open access MySpace profile called *The Chalks*, at Tom's house, for the
purpose of showcasing their band's material (Figure 3.2). On the day that I
interviewed the boys, they were composing and rehearsing a song to upload
to *The Chalks* profile page.

**Figure 3.2** The Chalks MySpace profile

Here, extracts from our discussion are described under headings in order to
explore how the critical digital literacy involved in profile page creation might
be viewed from an asset perspective.

## Positioning self in relation to others

Tom and Sam discuss in great detail how they manipulate their profile pages to achieve a desired effect. Tom and Sam have a strong understanding that profile pages can act to align or separate you from other people. As with most social network profile pages, *The Chalks* page has a space for *friends* to be featured. Friends are people who Tom and Sam have either accepted as contacts, following requests, or who Tom and Sam have requested to be added (Figure 3.3).

**Figure 3.3** The Chalks friends list

I asked Tom and Sam to categorize the friends shown on *The Chalks* profile page. They currently have only 14 friends: seven who have requested to be added, and seven who Sam and Tom have added themselves. They agreed that four categories of friends exist: *rejects* – the people whose requests they deny; *wanabees* – people who aspire to be associated with Tom and Sam for the social benefits that the association may bring; *genuine friends* – where Tom and Sam sense that the relationship is in balance; and *desirable friends* – the people who Tom and Sam want to be associated with in order to benefit themselves. The ability to categorize their *friends* in this way demonstrates a form of social mastery: the sense that who you are known to be friends with will impact upon the impression that you create online. Viewed from a critical digital literacy perspective, this demonstrates an explicit awareness of the potential for social engineering through text. In addition to the clear sense that who you know will impact on your positioning among others, Tom and Sam describe how the extent of the number of friends you have accumulated reflects your popularity, and contributes to the impression that you create. While Tom and Sam are not concerned about the number of friends featured on *The Chalks* profile, Tom boasts about the large number of friends included on his private profile. Here his *friends* list acts as a status symbol where friends become personal attributes; trophies of popularity supporting social positioning and affiliation.

## Silences and gaps

Unlike Clare's MySpace profile page, Tom and Sam are concerned to limit the representations of themselves on *The Chalks* profile to their uploaded music and a three-line description (see Figure 3.2). Pictures are excluded from the profile page, and only one blurred photograph of Tom is included in the *my pics* section of the site. Tom and Sam are discerning about the information they choose to include in *The Chalks* profile. They are aware that the profile will promote a certain image, and that by omitting information they are impacting on and controlling the image that they present. From a critical digital literacy perspective, this reflects that, as text producers, Tom and Sam have a clear sense that texts are made powerful by what is left out, as well as what is included.

## Intersection of online–offline contexts

Tom and Sam describe how friends create images for themselves through their profile pages to try to look 'cool' or 'sexy'. Tom admits to doing this in relation to his private profile. However, both boys are clear that your online profile, however 'cool', can easily be contradicted and uncovered by friends and contacts who are known at school and locally. The interconnectedness of the online textual and school worlds acts as a reality-checking mechanism. Tom and Sam have a clear sense that what happens in profile pages can become a hot topic for the playground. They are aware of the public nature of these texts and the wider implications of posting indiscriminately. The crossover from the digital textual landscape into school and beyond is described by Tom and Sam in detail, as they recount how a girl who posted a video of herself dancing in high heels became a source of amusement. According to Tom and Sam, the unfortunate girl attracted a large amount of negative interest in the playground as well as on her profile page. Tom and Sam easily distance themselves from this event as they talk critically about how this happened. Viewed from a critical digital literacy perspective, this example demonstrates how Tom and Sam see their texts as belonging to a much larger context that exceeds the boundaries of the online social network. This larger context is unregulated by privacy options, as children choose to discuss and show others examples that are otherwise inaccessible. Tom and Sam are aware of the implications of producing texts within this wider context, and act with caution to avoid becoming the source of negative interest themselves.

## Commercial and economic contexts

Drawing from his uncle's experience as a professional musician, and his understanding of the affordances and limitations offered by MySpace, Tom, in particular, is aware that *The Chalks* profile page has the potential to catapult the boys' music into the marketplace. Tom and Sam describe *The Chalks* profile page as a commercial venture: a space to promote their music to the widest possible audience. *The Chalks* is an open-access site, where anyone with access to the web address can visit. Recent performances of their band's music are featured here as a showcase. By publishing their music within this public arena, Tom and Sam are locating their text within a potentially global marketplace, and showing that they are beginning to recognize the implications for text within this wider commercial and economic context. The confidence to use text in this way demonstrates that Tom and Sam have moved beyond imagining a local audience for *The Chalks* profile page, and recognize the transformative potential of their text.

### Threat and safety

Tom and Sam believe that they are savvy users of MySpace, and at no threat from online bullying or grooming. Both boys are blasé about their online safety. They explain how MySpace users sometimes say that they are older than they are when online. To them this is an acceptable and even sensible measure. Their justification for giving a false age is that it helps to dissuade 'paedos' from becoming interested in them. For Tom and Sam, the threat of being pursued by a 'paedo' is something that they disregard with humour. For them, 'paedos' are 'out there', but pose no real threat. They assure me that they take heed of the stream of warnings about internet safety that pop up on their MySpace profile page. For Tom and Sam, keeping safe online is simply part of the everyday routine of social networking. Interestingly though, while Tom is dismissive about online predators posing a real threat to him, he is concerned that I and his parents should not view his private profile pages. These pages are for his friends only and are a forum for Tom to explore his representations of self beyond traditional safeguarding institutions. This sensitivity reflects a form of critical digital literacy, where Tom becomes empowered in relation to his parents by using the affordances of MySpace to subvert traditional power relations.

## Promoting critical digital literacy

These descriptions aim to provide glimpses of the sophisticated critical digital literacy that Tom and Sam possess, in order that we can begin to view children's text production in online spaces from an asset perspective. Clearly, these children are powerful and empowered subjects who are motivated to produce texts that are meaningful and of consequence for them. However, despite the achievements of children like Clare, Tom and Sam, a surge of concern around online social networking persists (DCSF, 2008; Ofcom, 2008). This concern is located mainly around children's safety from predators, and children's relative naiveté when posting potentially indiscriminate information about themselves in public and semi-public domains. The cause of this increasingly widespread concern can be attached to reports from the media, and the vigorous response from commercial and public sector bodies who are adopting responsibility for educating children and their families about how to stay safe online.[vii] A plethora of resources to educate parents, teachers and children about the safe use of the internet and social network sites are now widely available online and through school-based education programmes. These resources aim to enhance the safety of social networking as a recreational activity. However, they generally take the stance that children are at peril as their starting point. For example, the UK Information Commissioner's Office[viii] has published guidance for the safe use of social network sites, based on their belief that young people are unaware that future employers and educators may access these sites to covertly find out about individuals' histories (Information Commissioner's Office, 2007). Another high-profile resource for families and educators is the Child Exploitation and Online Protection Centre (CEOPC, 2007), a UK police agency that aims to work with parents and children to safeguard their online experiences. Both these well-intentioned resources position children as potential victims, in need of safeguarding. *The Byron Review: Children and New Technology* (DCSF, 2008), a current examination of children's behaviour in online spaces, takes a similar stance.

While these resources and reviews are extremely well intentioned, they provide a sense of the largely negative and protectionist frame that exists around children's digital text production in online spaces. This negative framing can be conceived as a reflection of the reportedly perilous context in which children create digital texts. Equally though, these resources can be regarded as an attempt by policy-makers to regain control over children's text production in digital landscapes. While these efforts are well meaning, there is a risk that this attempt to control online text production will actually fail to recognize and celebrate the creative, transformative and empowering energies that are being harnessed as children produce their own texts. For Clare, Tom and Sam, the creation of profile pages is not merely about skills and online safety. Instead, their critical digital literacy melds the notion of text production using new and evolving technologies with matters of social positioning in a wider social, cultural and economic context. For these children, the creation of texts in digital online contexts is fuelled, and only made meaningful, in relation to friendship, identity and social matters. Participation in online social networking, and collaboration around the act of producing and consuming texts online, contributes significantly to Clare and Tom's sense of who they are, what they do with their friends and how they fit in to their social worlds.

Based on these examples, it appears that the development and possession of critical digital literacy stems from children's experiences within both online and offline, local and global contexts. Participation in online social networking provides access to these interconnected contexts and allows the development of social as well as cultural, technological and academic mastery. For teachers to be able to support young people as producers of text within the widest range of textual landscapes, it appears that policy-makers and those responsible for educating and safeguarding children require an understanding of how the terms *literacy*, *digital literacy* and *critical digital literacy* can expand notions of text and text production in the twenty-first century. If these powerful groups can accept that it is insufficient to view children's text production as a merely skills-based and tested activity, or a subversive activity that needs to be safeguarded and controlled, children's online text production can cease to be framed in negative and protectionist ways. This chapter has attempted to demonstrate that children's digital text production in online spaces can be viewed from an asset perspective. By re-framing children's online text production as a positive and creative activity, the opportunity to develop children's critical digital literacy, and increasing mastery as effective and safe communicators in the twenty-first century, can only be enhanced.

## Notes

[i]  Bebo, MySpace and Facebook are popular social network sites. For an overview of social network sites, please see Boyd and Ellison (2007).

[ii]  *Digital footprint* is a term that is used to describe the online data trail created as owner-generated content is posted online. See the Pew Internet and American Life *Digital Footprints* report for further information www.pewinternet.org/PPF/r/229/report_display.asp

[iii]  See *The Children's Plan*, available online at www.dfes.gov.uk/publications/childrensplan/for the foreword by Ed Balls, Secretary of State for Children, Schools and Families.

[iv]  See *The Byron Review*, available online at www.dfes.gov.uk/byronreview/pdfs/Final%20Report%20Bookmarked.pdf for the foreword by Dr Tania Byron.

[v]  See the Labour Party 1997 Manifesto transcript available at www.bbc.co.uk/election97/background/parties/manlab/4lamanecon.html

[vi]  Wikipedia (2008) publishes a list of social network sites with user data. The sources are not published. See http://en.wikipedia.org/wiki/List_of_social_network_websites

[vii]  A Google search for 'children's safety online' identifies over 41 million hits. See www.google.com/search?sourceid=navclient&ie=UTF-8&&q=children%27s+safety+online

[viii] The Information Commissioner's Office is the UK's independent authority set up to promote access to official information and to protect personal information. For details see www.ico.gov.uk/

## References

Alexa. (2008) *Top Sites: United Kingdom*. Retrieved 17 January 2008, from www.alexa.com/site/ds/top_sites?cc=GB&ts_mode=country&lang=none

Barton, D. and Hamilton, M. (2000) 'Literacy practices', in D. Barton, M. Hamilton and R. Ivanic (eds), *Situated Literacies*. London: Routledge

*BBC Panorama: One Click from Danger* (2007) Programme broadcast 21 December, Jeremy Vine, reporter. Retrieved 21 December 2007, from http://news.bbc.co.uk/1/hi/programmes/panorama/7107918.stm

Bearne, E. (2003) 'Rethinking literacy; communication, representation and text', *Reading, Literacy and Language*, 37(3): 98–103.

Bearne, E. (2005) 'Interview with Gunther Kress', *Discourse: Studies in the Cultural Politics of Education*, 26(3): 287–99.

Boyd, D. (2007) 'Why youth love social network sites: the role of networked publics in teenage social life', in D. Buckingham (ed.), *MacArthur Foundation Series on Digital Learning – Youth, Identity, and Digital Media Volume*. Cambridge, MA: MIT Press.

Boyd, D.M. and Ellison, N.B. (2007) 'Social network sites: definition, history, and scholarship', *Journal of Computer-Mediated Communication*, 13(1), art. 11. Retrieved 17 January 2008, from http://jcmc.indiana.edu/vol13/issue1/boyd.ellison.html

Carrington, V. (2005) 'New textual landscapes', in J. Marsh (ed.), *Popular Culture, New Media and Digital Literacy in Early Childhood*. Oxford: RoutledgeFalmer.

Child Exploitation and Online Protection Centre (CEOPC) (2007) Retrieved 21 February 2008, from www.ceop.gov.uk/

Childnet International (2007a) *digizen.org: What are Social Networking Services?* Retrieved 14 February 2008, from www.digizen.org/socialnetworking/what.aspx#3

Childnet International (2007b) *digizen.org: what makes you such a good digizen?* Retrieved 14 February 2008, from www.digizen.org/socialnetwork/

Davies, J. (2007) 'Display, identity and the everyday: self-presentation through online image sharing', *Discourse: Studies in the Cultural Politics of Education*, 28(4): 549–64.

Department for Children, Schools and Families (DCSF) (2007). *The Children's Plan*. London: HMSO. Retrieved 22 May 2008, from www.dfes.gov.uk/publications/childrensplan/downloads/The_Childrens_Plan.pdf

Department for Children, Schools and Families (DCSF) (2008) *The Byron Review: Children and New Technology*. Retrieved 14 November 2007, from www.dfes.gov.uk/byronreview/

Department for Education and Employment (DfEE) (1998) *The National Literacy Strategy Framework for Teaching*. London: DfEE

Department for Education and Employment/Qualifications and Curriculum Authority (1999) *The National Curriculum for England: English*. London: The Stationery Office.

Department for Education and Skills (DfES) (2006) *Primary National Strategy: Primary Framework for Literacy and Mathematics*. London: DfES.

Dobson, T. and Willinsky, J. (in press) 'Digital literacy', in D. Olson and N. Torrence (eds), *The Cambridge Handbook of Literacy*. Retrieved 25 January 2008, from http://pkp.sfu.ca/files/Digital%20Literacy.pdf

Dowdall, C. (2006) 'Dissonance between the digitally created words of school and home', *Literacy*, 40(3): 153–63.

Freebody, P. and Luke, A. (1990) 'Literacies programs: debates and demands in cultural context', *Prospect: Australian Journal of TESOL*, 5(7): 7–16.

Freire, P. and Macedo, D. (1987) *Literacy: Reading the Word and the World*. Hadley, MA: Bergin and Garvey.

Gee, J.P. (1996) *An Introduction to Discourse Analysis*. London: Routledge.

Gee, J.P. (2003) *What Computer Games Have to Teach Us about Learning and Literacy*. Basingstoke: Palgrave Macmillan.

Goffman, E. (1959) *The Presentation of Self in Everyday Life*. Garden City, NY: Doubleday.

Grainger, T. (2004) 'Introduction: travelling across the terrain', in T. Grainger (ed.), *The RoutledgeFalmer Reader in Literacy*. London: RoutledgeFalmer.

Information Commissioner's Office (2007) Social Networking. Retrieved 13 December 2008, from www.ico.gov.uk/for_the_public/topic_specific_guides/social_networking.aspx

Kress, G. (2003) *Literacy in the New Media Age*. London: Routledge.

Liu, H. (2007) 'Social network profiles as taste performances', *Journal of Computer-Mediated Communication*, 13(1), art. 13. Retrieved 4 February 2008, from http://jcmc.indiana.edu/vol13/issue1/liu.html

Livingstone, S. and Bober, M. (2005) *UK Children Go Online: Final Report of Key Project Findings*. April. London: LSE Report. Retrieved 19 January 2008, from www.children-go-online.net

Livingstone, S. and Haddon, L. (2007) *EU Kids Online*. Retrieved 19 January 2008, from www.lse.ac.uk/collections/EUKidsOnline/

Luke, A. and Carrington, V. (2002) 'Globalisation, literacy, curriculum practice', in R. Fisher, M. Lewis and G. Brooks (eds), *Raising Standards in Literacy*. London: RoutledgeFalmer.

Luke, A. and Freebody, P. (1999) 'Further notes on the Four Resources Model', *Reading Online*. Retrieved 22 May 2008, from www.readingonline.org/research/lukefreebody. html#freebodyluke

Marsh, J. (2005) 'Children of the Digital Age', in J. Marsh (ed.), *Popular Culture, New Media and Digital Literacy in Early Childhood*. Oxford: RoutledgeFalmer.

Marsh, J., Brooks, G., Hughes, J., Ritchie, L., Roberts, S. and Wright, K. (2005) *Digital Beginnings: Young Children's Use of Popular Culture, Media and New Technologies*. Retrieved 24 January 2008, from www.digitalbeginnings.shef.ac.uk/DigitalBeginningsReport.pdf

Martin, A. (2006) *Digital Literacy Needed in an 'e-permeated' World: Progress Report of DigEuLit Project*. Retrieved 17 February 2008, from www.elearningeuropa.info/directory/ index.php?page=doc&doc_id=6973&doclng=6

National Statistics (2008) *Internet Access*. Retrieved 11 January 2008, from www. statistics.gov.uk/CCI/nugget.asp?ID=8&Pos=1&ColRank=1&Rank=192

New London Group. (1996) 'A pedagogy of multiliteracies: designing social futures', *Harvard Educational Review*, 66(1): 60–92.

Office for Standards in Education (Ofsted) (2003) *Yes He Can: Schools Where Boys Write Well*. London: HMI.

Office of Communications (Ofcom) (2007) *Communications Market Reports 2007: Key Points*. Retrieved 11 January 2008, from www.ofcom.org.uk/research/cm/cmr07/keypoints/

Office of Communications (Ofcom) (2008) *Social Networking: A Quantitative and Qualitative Research Report into Attitudes, Behaviour and Use*. Retrieved 22 May 2008, from www.ofcom.org.uk/advice/media_literacy/medlitpub/medlitpubrss/socialnetworking/ report.pdf

Pahl, K. (2007) 'Creativity in events and practices: a lens for understanding children's multimodal texts', *Literacy*, 41(2): 86–92.

Pahl, K. and Rowsell, J. (2005) *Literacy and Education*. London: Paul Chapman Publishing.

Pew Internet and American Life Project (2007) *Digital Footprints: Online Identity Management and Search in the Age of Transparency*. Retrieved 3 February 2008, from www.pewinternet.org/pdfs/PIP_Digital_Footprints.pdf

Qualifications and Curriculum Authority (QCA) (2004) *More than Words: Multimodal Texts in the Classroom*. London: QCA.

Qualifications and Curriculum Authority (QCA) (2005) *More than Words 2: Creating Stories on Page and Screen*. London: QCA.

Street, B.V. (ed.) (1993) *Cross Cultural Approaches to Literacy*. Cambridge: Cambridge University Press.

United Kingdom Literacy Association/Primary National Strategy (UKLA/PNS) (2004) *Raising Boys' Achievements in Writing*. Retrieved 19 August 2007, from www.standards.dfes. gov.uk/primary/publications/literacy/1094843/pns_ukla_boys094304report.pdf

Wenger, E. (1998) *Communities of Practice, Learning, Meaning and Identity*. Cambridge: Cambridge University Press.

Wikipedia (2008) *List of Social Network Sites*. Retrieved 15 January 2008, from http://en.wikipedia.org/wiki/List_of_social_network_websites

Younger, M. and Warrington, M. (2005) *Raising Boys' Achievements*. London: DfES.

# Download

## Key points

1. Children's text production beyond the classroom is frequently framed in negative and protectionist ways. Instead of celebrating children's creativity as text producers in online social network sites, children's activities as text producers are at risk from being stifled by concerned parties and a surrounding discourse of concern.
2. Discussion with three children about their online text production has highlighted that a range of social, cultural, technological and academic masteries govern their use of profile pages. These masteries exceed those that are demanded by the school curriculum for text production, as the context for online text production connects both online and offline, local and global issues.
3. Teachers have the opportunity to recognize the full range of masteries that children must harness in order to communicate successfully in the twenty-first century using a range of textual forms. The promotion of children's *critical digital literacy* should become the remit of teachers in order to begin to re-frame children's text production from an asset perspective.

## In your classroom

1. Invite children to lead a discussion exploring how social network sites are used to produce texts for a range of reasons.
2. Research available television documentaries and online resources about social networking (for example, BBC *Panorama: One click from Danger*, 2007; Child Exploitation and Online Protection Centre, 2007; *The Byron Review: A Summary for Children and Young People*). From a critical literacy perspective, discuss how these texts position young people in relation to social networking and suggest alternative readings.
3. Develop children's awareness of the range of masteries that are required in order to communicate successfully and positively in online contexts. Prepare material for a website to publish positive guidance for social networking.

## Further reading

Boyd, D.M. and Ellison, N.B. (2007) 'Social network sites: definition, history, and scholarship', *Journal of Computer-Mediated Communication*, 13(1), art. 11. Retrieved 17 January 2008, from http://jcmc.indiana.edu/vol13/issue1/ boyd.ellison.html

Digizen/BECTA (2007) *Young People and Social Network Sites*. Retrieved 21 January 2008, from www.digizen.org/socialnetwork/

Office of Communications (Ofcom) (2008) *Social Networking: A Quantitative and Qualitative Research Report into Attitudes, Behaviour and Use*. Retrieved 22 May 2008, from www.ofcom.org.uk/advice/media

# Part B

# Changing literacies

The research in this section focuses most specifically on the ways in which digital texts, and the technologies that enable them to be produced and accessed, are folded into the formalized learning communities of classrooms to unsettle traditional models of knowledge transmission. These chapters explore the implications of wikis for the ways in which young people engage with text and information; consider the use of blogging as a way to understand the dynamic nature of online texts, and the skills and practices that can be developed in classrooms through their use; and take a first look at the use of 3D online environments for literacy teaching. This section provides a showcase of the ways in which in- and out-of-classroom practices with digital text can be productively linked, and the types of challenges and innovations that may arise. Readers are encouraged to reflect on how these instances of digital literacy practices might inform their own practice in different contexts and with different age groups.

# From Wikipedia to the Humble Classroom Wiki: Why We Should Pay Attention to Wikis

## *Victoria Carrington*

> Author: a person who composes a book, article, or other written work.

> Encyclopedia: a work that contains information on all branches of knowledge or treats comprehensively a particular branch of knowledge usually in articles arranged alphabetically often by subject.

## Introduction

A small boy – let's call him James[i] – is in an early childhood classroom. He is a little over five years of age. James has just finished creating a story – with his new set of crayons bought for just that purpose – that intricately weaves the picture he has drawn with the invented spelling of his single line of print. His teacher congratulates him, asks that he read it aloud and then suggests that he write his name on it, 'so we know who it *belongs* to'. Without hesitation, James picks up a crayon and carefully writes his name 'James' in the top left-hand corner. At the close of the school day, James proudly takes his piece of text home to show his parents and other family members. Once again his ownership and authority is reinforced as he reads his story and points out the finer details of his proto-signature. It is clear that this cute five-year-old 'owns' this piece of printed text and that it is complete. James is an *author*.

Foucault (1977) reminds us that while we tend to consider it to be a taken for granted, the idea of the author is historically located and relational. As Foucault suggested, James's vision of himself as an author and owner of his printed text is historically and culturally positioned rather than universal. In this it is linked to a set of historical, cultural, and economic intersections that have their source as far back as the 15th century and the development of printing-press technology. In the very early 1960s Marshall McLuhan (1962) published *The Gutenberg Galaxy* and mounted the technologically determinist argument that movable type is the 'ground zero' of modern Western notions of individualism, nation and capitalism. While overstating the causal role of the printing press, McLuhan noted the strong interconnection between available technologies and the kinds of social, cultural, political and economic practices that emerge alongside. He argued that the means of communication has an impact beyond the message contained within it, and thus the technology of the printing press and the distribution processes that grew up alongside it (static paper pages, bookbinding, mail and road/rail transport, unit-based commercial purchase and sale) had an impact. The connection of movable print type with emergent capitalism and an individualist ideology resonates with the emergence of *the author* in the modern moral imaginary. Immersed in this tradition and against the backdrop of social institutions that reflect many of these trends, James's role and rights as an author appear incontrovertible and unproblematic to him, and to the adults and social institutions around him.

However, the 15th century is distant in time and technology. Printing-press technology and the static print it produces are no longer the only medium with which the important texts of our culture are created and distributed. The emergence of digital technologies has enabled the development and use of a range of digital texts, many of which are enabling practices that challenge the informational and moral economies built around print text. Some of these texts, including wikis, do not celebrate or even recognize authorship or ownership in the ways in which they are understood in relation to printed text. This chapter attends to this shift and explores the varied impacts and affordances of wikis and their possible role as litmus test for larger cultural shift around the way in which text production and information are culturally positioned. Specifically, it considers the emblematic online collaborative encyclopedia, *Wikipedia*, and a range of classroom-based wikis. To set the scene for this discussion, the chapter first briefly looks at the ways in which notions of childhood are closely entwined with other social themes including technology, access to information and a peculiarly linear view of human development.

## Technology change, childhood and children

The history of the printing press demonstrates that there is a highly complex relationship between the development of various technologies and their take up and use by individuals and groups. Like all other technological change, interactive technologies have emerged alongside other broader social, cultural and political reorganization. However, the way in which we perceive and represent children and young people allows us to pinpoint key areas of instability and tension. One technological determinist view represents contemporary children as increasingly 'active' and 'worldly' because there are now technologies that enable and encourage this. Another prominent determinist view is that young people, inundated with undifferentiated information, are increasingly uncritical and undiscerning. The reality is, not surprisingly, more complicated. Movies, television and video games reflect the tensions around childhood and adulthood in contemporary Western cultures. In the 1990s the *Home Alone* movie franchise spoke to the emergence of what was then called a 'postmodern' childhood, providing a commentary on the shifting sands of adult–child competence and the boundaries. In a similar manner, the US sitcom *Two and a Half Men* problematizes issues of maturity and masculinity; reality television show *Kid Nation* created a society without adults and televised the outcome; and the behaviour of teenaged and young adult star/lets, including the ways in which they are exploited by the media, also, to some degree, exemplifies the diffusion of adult–child expectations and roles (for example, the 24/7 intense scrutiny of Britney Spears' every move by a phalanx of paparazzi).

The printing press heralded an information revolution that drew from and enabled other social, cultural and political change. It was a technology of its time. A growing segment of the public were able to access information in volumes and types never previously imagined, challenging the traditional authority of the church and scholars. Apprenticeship in print literacy was also about immersion into a particular moral imaginary that worked to shape what is thinkable and unthinkable, our assumptions, dispositions and prejudices (Jantzen, 2001). While the diversity of books expanded, the affordances of print acted to solidify or standardize facts and information and, concomitantly, the role and rights of the author became increasingly prominent, forming part of the moral economy. At the same time, the emergence of the printing press has been associated with the development of the 20th century notions of adulthood and childhood that still hold sway in curriculum, learning theory, and media discourses. Postman (1994) makes the argument that:

> the modern idea of adulthood is largely a product of the printing press. Almost all of the characteristics we associate with adulthood are those that are (and were) either generated or amplified by the requirements of a fully literate culture: the capacity for self-restraint, a tolerance for delayed gratification, a sophisticated ability to think conceptually and sequentially, a preoccupation with both historical continuity and the future, a high valuation of reason and hierarchical order. (pp. 98–9)

Noting the dependent relationship between constructs of adult and child, Postman suggests that childhood is a social construction premised on developmental and sequential access to information. The lengthy apprenticeship in learning to read and write in order to access information is linked, in this view, to maturation and the path to adulthood. In the 1980s, Postman and others expressed deep concern that television's undifferentiated content and broadcast media was eroding the division between adulthood and childhood. Postman (1982) argued that television required no instruction, made no complex demands and did not differentiate audiences, and as a consequence 'eroded' the division that had traditionally existed. Undifferentiated broadcast media did not respect the established differences between children, allowing children to access information that had once been limited to adults.

Beyond Postman, much has been written about the rise and decline of 20th century Euro-American notions of 'childhood' (see, for example, Aries, 1962; Carrington, 2005; Steinberg and Kincheloe, 1997; Tapscott, 1998). This was a childhood lived within the confines of the gendered nuclear family, modernist institutional schooling and the suburban tracts made possible by the cultural dominance of the automobile. Much of the impetus for the decline of this model of childhood has been laid at the door of interactive media and the increasing ability of children and adolescents to access a wide array of uncensored and unmediated information, as well as 'adult' entertainment. Postman's 'secrets' are increasingly exposed to children, and, as a result, the ways in which childhood is understood and enacted are seen to be shifting. The tensions attached to these changes play out across a range of forums from alarmist reports of youth crime, drug use and sexual activity, to claims of declining literacy and disengagement from schooling. Childhood has become a battleground where larger issues are redefined and fought. Jenkins's (1992) notion of the 'politics of substitution' proposes that children are invoked to focus attention on moral panics: concern with homosexuality becomes redefined as concern with paedophilia; campaigns focused on pornography are reshaped around the notion of child pornography; broader concern with public health coalesces around childhood obesity. These moral panics tend to coalesce around children and young people and, in particular, their capacity to access pornography, violence and other 'unsavoury' information. For many, there are concerns that young people do not have the skills to fend off predators, and that they do not have the skills to critically assess the validity and source of the information they come across online. Linked to this, the ability of children and young people to upload information independent of adult mediation and supervision is also cause for concern. Buckingham (2000) argues that the tension around childhood centres on issues of access and control and this can be seen playing out in these discourses. Young children are depicted as prone to displaying too much personal information on their personal sites and/or meeting strangers, which, in turn, puts them at risk in the online environment. Again, sexual predation and other forms of exploitation are constructed as a permanent and direct risk. Each of these panics is premised on a deficit view of young people and their capacities to engage independently with a new technology, new social interactions and new forms of textual practice. These discourses of panic and risk also link back to the dependent relationship between constructions of childhood and adulthood. Depictions of children and young people as deficit and immature cannot be disassociated from the traditional view of adults as complete – as mature and responsible citizens with defined role identities and trajectories. However, learning to be literate – to participate in contemporary culture in ways that are effective – requires practices with technologies and text that are qualitatively different than those attached to print literacy and the moral economies that surrounded it. The remainder of this chapter constitutes an examination of the emergence and affordances of wikis in light of this shifting ground.

## Wikipedia

Wiki – it is well known that the word itself is drawn from the Hawaiian term 'wiki wiki' indicating something that is quick. It is 'a type of website that allows anyone visiting the site to add, remove as well as edit all content, quickly and easily' (http://en.Wikipedia.org/wiki/Wiki). Wikis, in all their forms, allow online asynchronous editing of documents without mastery of programming languages. The particular affordances of the associated software have meant that wikis are sites of collaborative writing and editing; it is possible for multiple writers to collaboratively write and edit a piece of text, save and compare versions of the document, embed hypertext links and upload attachments. Leuf and Cunningham (2001) called this capacity *open editing*. The software that allows this collaborative textual construction also compiles an ongoing archive of each version of the wiki as changes are made.

Of all the wikis active online, *Wikipedia*, the free, online encyclopedia, is far and away the most famous. From a starting point in 2001, up to April 2007, 5.77 million Wikipedians had used 236 million separate edits to build a network of 6.4 million articles written in 250 languages (Wilkinson and Huberman, 2007). It is, without doubt, a phenomenon. *Wikipedia*, at its best, is a grand social experiment. The *Wikipedia* introductory page provides a first window onto the operational philosophy and purpose of the site:

> Wikipedia is an encyclopedia collaboratively written by many of its readers. It is a special type of website, called a wiki, that makes collaboration easy. Many people are constantly improving Wikipedia, making thousands of changes an hour, all of which are recorded on article histories and recent changes. Inappropriate changes are usually removed quickly, and repeat offenders can be blocked from editing. If you add new material to Wikipedia, please provide references. Facts that are unreferenced are routinely removed from the encyclopedia. ... You can't break Wikipedia. Anything can be fixed or improved later. (http://en.wikipedia.org/wiki/Wikipedia:About)

Encyclopedias are, of course, not a new phenomenon, and interestingly they have often been controversial, particularly when their emergence coincided with other tensions. Diderot's eighteenth-century encyclopedic bestseller *Encyclopédie, ou dictionnaire raisonné des sciences, des arts et des métiers* (*Encyclopedia, or Classified Dictionary of Sciences, Arts, and Trades*) was feared and reviled by French religious and political figures who labelled it as highly dangerous. It purposefully foregrounded human reason and science at the expense of other forms of knowledge and truth, directly challenging the orthodoxy of the mainstream Church and marking the philosophical and intellectual shift that paved the way for the era in which we now live. As Darnton (1988, p. 2) notes: 'as a physical object and as a vehicle of ideas, The *Encyclopédie* synthesized a thousand arts and sciences; it represented the Enlightenment, body and soul'. The compilation and distribution of this early encyclopedia was as much a political act as a literary one and reflected new patterns of thought and participation along with available technologies. It was very much of its time. The same could be said of *Wikipedia*.

For wikis in general, and *Wikipedia* in particular, to become culturally valued textual practices they must be embedded in larger changes. What has been termed a 'participatory culture' (Jenkins et al., 2006) has grown up around the use of new digital technologies and the opportunities they allow for individuals and groups to create, share and distribute their own content and multimodal productions. The momentum around increasing participation across a range of forums is making it ever more valuable to be able to create multimodal texts that operate across a range of media platforms, to rapidly critique information from a range of sources, to move back and forward between basic skills in print literacies and skills in multiliteracies, and to work in peer learning contexts and informal settings. In this context, *Wikipedia* has also connected to a participatory Zeitgeist. In an era where digital technologies are increasingly embedded in the everyday, and where many of the valued and rewarded practices of government, corporation and popular culture are those associated with these skill-sets, effective and successful economic and civic participation are crucially tied to mastery of digital technologies and engagement with participatory culture. Jenkins (2006) contends that in the contemporary cultural and technological landscape, participation is an important political right. The skills of effective and ethical participation become, in this view, crucial to effective citizenship and engagement. Jenkins (2006) makes a link between participatory culture and *Wikipedia*, making the case that it is premised upon a 'moral economy of information' (p. 255). Jenkins (2006, p. 254) suggests that,

> perhaps the most interesting and controversial aspect of the Wikipedia project has been the ways it shifts what counts as knowledge (from the kinds of topics sanctioned by traditional encyclopedias to a much broader range of topics of interest to specialized interest groups and subcultures) and the ways it shifts what counts as expertise (from recognized academic authorities to something close to Levy's concept of collective intelligence).

Jenkins (2006) argues that *Wikipedia* works because increasing numbers of people are embracing their obligations as participants in a community.

Traditional print-based encyclopedias were themselves premised on a moral economy of information – the furore about Diderot's encyclopedia was linked to the ways in which it both reflected and contributed to the Enlightenment's shift of authority and knowledge from institutional religion to science – but one that was different in many ways from the economy that underwrites *Wikipedia* and participatory culture. However, the *Wikipedia* experiment and the ways in which it challenges more traditional moral and informational economies and participation are not universally applauded. BBC Radio 4 sums up general concerns when it asks 'Is Wikipedia a valuable source of human knowledge or a symptom of the spread of mediocrity and the devaluation of research?' (Anderson, 2007). A UK academic recently used her inaugural professorial lecture to call the search engine Google 'white bread for the mind' and added that students 'live in an age of information, but what they lack is correct information. They turn to Wikipedia unquestioningly for information' (Frean,

2008). Many of the following critiques focus on the use of online information sources by the young:

- *Should students be banned from using Google and Wikipedia?*
  http://blogs.guardian.co.uk/digitalcontent/2008/01/should_students_be_banned_from.html
- *White bread for young minds, says university professor*
  http://technology.timesonline.co.uk/tol/news/tech_and_web/the_web/article3182091.ece
- *Wikipedia banned by Middlebury College for history students*
  http://blog.historians.org/news/123/Wikipedia-banned-by-middlebury-college-for-history-students
- *A stand against Wikipedia*
  www.insidehighered.com/news/2007/01/26/wiki

In each of these articles, *Wikipedia* is represented as an inferior source of information and its use is linked to a perceived deficit in the young: they are not achieving; they are lazy; they are not critical; and they do not appreciate the significance of traditional forms of knowledge. They are changing, moving away from established standards. There is a clear concern that the young (rather than adults) are developing a non-hierarchical view of information, have easy access to too much information and are not critical enough. While many media headlines begin with 'Wikipedia banned', further investigation often reveals that the majority of educational institutions require that all encyclopedia and all virtual information be verified by the use of other sources. As always, good research protocol includes multiple sources, cross-referencing, and critical reading. Ready access to a free, online encyclopedia does not change this. However, *change* is very much at the heart of concerns around *Wikipedia*.

It is clear that issues of accuracy and expertise are also central to the controversies swirling around *Wikipedia*. In 2005, after much media speculation, the science journal *Nature* published the results of their survey of the comparative accuracy of the *Encyclopaedia Britannica* (online edition) and *Wikipedia*. The article reported that there was little effective difference in accuracy between the free, co-operative *Wikipedia* and the subscription service expertly created *Encyclopaedia Britannica*. The furore over this finding was instructive. *Encyclopaedia Britannica* took out a not inexpensive half-page advertisement in *The Times* demanding a retraction of the *Nature* story and its central claims. *Nature* refused. These themes are also reflected in the following media headlines, which focus on Wikipedia's validity and reliability:

- 'Fake professor in Wikipedia storm',
  http://news.bbc.co.uk/2/hi/americas/6423659.stm
- 'Wikipedia "shows CIA page edits"',
  http://news.bbc.co.uk/2/hi/technology/6947532.stm
- 'Japanese workers in Wikipedia row',
  http://news.bbc.co.uk/2/hi/asia-pacific/7029685.stm

- 'Howard row over Wikipedia edits',
  http://news.bbc.co.uk/2/hi/asia-pacific/7029685.stm
- 'Wiked Pedia alterations',
  http://www.theaustralian.news.com.au/story/0,25197,22264548–26397,00.html

Linked to these issues of expertise and accuracy – which speak to trustworthiness and validity, and therefore authority – there are also heated debates about the quality and significance of the knowledge and facts included in the millions of entries. A recent example can be tracked through the Australian news media. In early 2008, community discussion was sparked by the rise to media notoriety of a Sydney teenager who held a party that required police helicopters, police dogs and squad cars to break up. The headlines track the story as it developed, moved online and, finally, sparked *Wikipedia* community debate:

- '500 teens rampage as police end party', *The Australian*, 14 January 2008.
- 'Experts blame folks for party boy's actions', *The Australian*, 19 January 2008.
- 'MySpace party boy makes world headlines', *The Australian*, 15 January 2008.
- 'Wikipedia rejects Corey entry', *The Australian*, 16 January 2008.
- 'Wikipedia users reject Corey Delaney entry', *News.com.au*, 16 January 2008.
- 'Web starts to turn on party boy', *The Australian*, 17 January 2008.
- 'Corey kicked off Wikipedia a second time', *News.com.au*, 13 February 2008.

Issues of quality, validity, significance and security underpin much of the public debate over this new encyclopedia. However, what also underlies criticism of *Wikipedia* is a sense of unease with the practices and attitudes attached to it. Key to *Wikipedia* is participation. People take the time to contribute, read and edit *Wikipedia* entries. Cover (2004, p. 174) argues that 20th century media are defined by linearity and a 'fixed idea of authorship, text and audience'. He argues that:

> [the] rise of interactivity as a form of audience participation is by no means the latest trend in media history nor something that disrupts a prior synergy between author-text-audience, but a strongly held and culturally based desire to participate in the creation and transformation of the text that has effectively been denied by previous technologies of recorded media production and distribution. (2004, p. 174)

Assuming that Cover (2004) and Jenkins et al. (2006) are correct and we are moving into a participatory culture, *Wikipedia* is an impressive example of collective intelligence and community commitment. This in itself is unique; a bottom-up encyclopedia that challenges the role of the expert to create knowledge. *Wikipedia* also manages to challenge existing corporate models. The traditional print encyclopedia has always been a commercial enterprise. Diderot's original printed encyclopedia had to be purchased, and even now online access to *Encyclopaedia Britannica* is by subscription (see www.britannica.com). Access to *Wikipedia* is free to anyone with the necessary digital access.

Importantly, the culture in which *Wikipedia* thrives is shifting the relationship between expertise, the right to create and distribute texts, and the role of the author. This has significant implications for classroom literacy practices, including the conceptual frame in which literacy takes place and interactions between teachers and students. I begin to explore these in the section below.

## Wikis in the classroom

The ease of set-up and low cost have made wikis a popular choice in many classrooms engaging with digital culture, in the UK, the USA, Australia and elsewhere. Their relative novelty still carries enough cachet to give them credibility, and the vast range of uses make them malleable yet unobtrusive. The ways in which wikis are used in classrooms are, of course, as varied as the classrooms themselves. However, an online survey of classroom wikis from the UK and the USA[ii] enables a set of core uses to be identified (see Table 4.1). A selection of these core uses is discussed here.

**Table 4.1**  Core uses for wikis

| Category | Key features |
| --- | --- |
| Knowledge management | Home page/classroom information hub with range of linked pages: class assignments, rubrics, individual pages, subject pages, tutorials |
| Narrative builder | Collaborative construction of text; feedback on individual text via discussion feature of wiki; use of wiki pages to create 'choose your own pathway' stories |
| Resource aggregator | List of, and external links to, a range of themed resources |
| Value adding | Use of links, glossaries to add density; value add pieces of existing text. |

*Room 4's wiki* (http://room4-wiki.wikispaces.com/) is, in effect, an extended collaborative narrative in the psycholinguistic tradition of shared writing that allows the teacher to foreground a range of story writing conventions. Their wiki home page has an image of a group of Grade Two students sitting on the floor of their classroom with the caption, 'We are learning how to write, so this page was created to allow us to write and edit together. Below is our study in progress'. A story about a boy called Nolan who plays hockey is under construction, becoming longer with each edit. The story has a single photo of an ice hockey game embedded into the opening paragraph. The remainder of the lengthy, and growing, story is text and linear in structure. *GVC 2006–07 TEAM 06* is also using their wiki to produce a collaborative superhero story, across schools in Arizona, Illinois and Quebec, for a contest (http://gvc06.wikispaces.com/). Taking a different approach, *Glengarrypedia* (http://glengarrypedia.wikispaces.com/) used the affordances of wiki software to enable students to build a class glossary for key cultural references associated with a class novel. Each entry has a range of external links and references as well as an uploaded image. Another category of wiki sites is comprised of those made by teachers for teachers. Developed as sites for sharing resources, these tend to be composed of a single wiki page with lists of external links to resources (see, for example, http://wvmentorteacher.pbwiki.com/ or http://theconnectedclassroom.wikispaces.com/). Many of these wikis and their external links are thematic. That is, they are discipline-based, focusing on mathematics or poetry, for example, or they focus on thematic topics, such as mentoring, middle schooling or behavior management, for example.

Other classrooms use their wiki as an information hub (see http://westwood.wikispaces.com/). In this context, the wiki becomes the site where homework is posted, where assignments are listed and where students upload various pieces of work. The wiki is a central point for accessing and disseminating information; for drawing students and teachers together in a community space unhindered by distance and time (see Figure 4.1).

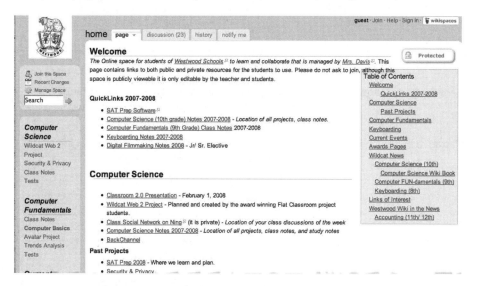

**Figure 4.1** The Westwood wiki

Often, these wikis feature abundant links to additional information: software tutorials, in-depth information on a topic, assessment rubrics, troubleshooting. One of the best – the award-winning Flat Classroom Project – has pages titled 'What should I be doing?' and 'Don't Panic!' as well as 'Let your teacher know when you're having trouble connecting' (http://flatclassroomproject.wikispaces.com/). It takes advantage of the affordances of Web 2.0 technologies to create a network of teachers and students, in diverse geographic locations, who all contribute to the wiki. On one level, the wiki is directed at students and in some ways takes on many of the day-to-day organizational tasks that a teacher traditionally spends time on – restating assignments, identifying tasks, sharing new information among students and giving feedback. On another, it provides opportunities for independent work and task management by students. While acting as a core hub, *FlatClassroomProject* moves a step further by assuming, as a first principle, that students will create information for use by colleagues in a range of sites. Another classroom wiki, *Room15wiki*, has video mathematics tutorials created and uploaded by students (http://mrlindsay.pbwiki.com/). In a linked wiki page, the teacher and a range of students provide feedback (in different coloured fonts) to a student's movie review. This classroom wiki is an attempt to create an online community and to value student produced information.

These wikis can productively be analysed along a continuum towards increasing engagement with the principles of participatory culture (see Figure 4.2). While all the uses of classroom wikis described here are commendable, they are located in the first two spheres of activity, moving from a focus on maintaining traditional classroom practices, through to aggregating external links, and on to active networking and incorporation of student-created content. Each usage style reflects differences in community, school infrastructure and leadership, access to the necessary digital technologies, and teacher expertise and interest.

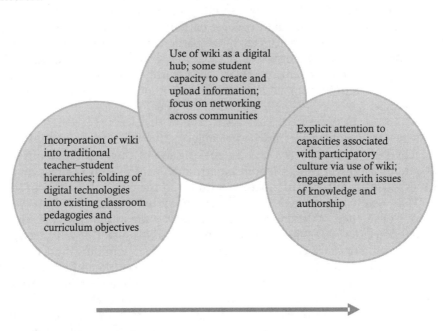

**Figure 4.2** Continuum of engagement with wikis

The ways in which wikis are taken up and used in classrooms are also dependent on how teachers interpret the world outside the classroom. For teachers who perceive a shift towards increasing participation and the deeper embedding of digital technologies in work and social landscapes, it is likely there will be a greater priority placed on working towards the more complex skills, capacities and attitudes associated with the notion of participatory culture (see

Graham, 2008). According to Jenkins et al. (2006) these form the 'hidden curriculum' of effective participation in contemporary workplaces and social contexts: the ability to experiment and take risks; the ability to improvise and adopt different identities and stances; the capacity to appropriate and remix media and cultural content; the ability to take fluid and flexible perspectives on issues and tasks; the capacity to work collaboratively and to negotiate across an array of contexts; the ability and attitudes necessary to synthesize and evaluate information from a range of sources. This is the broader context in which *Wikipedia* has risen to global prominence. There are increased opportunities for, and a cultural momentum towards, participation: via amateur production, the ability to redo and edit, risk-taking, and online interaction and mentoring. The skills and attitudes that provide young people with opportunities to participate effectively in this world are often not the skills and attitudes rewarded in our school system. Teachers would be wise to pay attention to this hidden curriculum of participation (Jenkins et al., 2006), to the features of wikis that allow opportunities for new forms of participation and to the broader context in which they are coming to prominence. This hidden curriculum is also the reason that schools and education bureaucracies should be ensuring that all children have opportunities to engage with print *and* digital texts for a range of purposes. If classroom wikis are to evolve patterns of use that more closely link to the kinds of practices that characterize participatory culture, teachers must be supported in a number of ways: first, to engage with this culture; secondly, to develop the kinds of skills necessary; and thirdly, provided with sufficient time and resourcing to embed them into curriculum in meaningful and sustainable ways.

The evidence assembled for this chapter suggests that while increasing numbers of teachers are aware of wikis and are making use of them in classroom contexts, they are not yet using them in ways that reflect the array of practices and attitudes identified with participatory culture. On the whole, the types of practices that have characterized the growth and contestations around *Wikipedia* are not in evidence. With few exceptions, the way classroom wikis are used is linked to lower-level use, taking advantage of an easy-to-use, free web page, and reflects older models of childhood. Practices such as scaffolding students into the skills and attitudes of participatory culture with online and offline texts, developing and modelling new relationships around teacher–student authority and knowledge patterns and designing new pedagogies to match, or explicitly engaging with the contingent nature of text and information, are not so much in evidence. While these activities may take place offline in the physical spaces of the classroom, with a few exceptions, they are not yet reflected in the design or operation of classroom-based wikis. However, there is reason to feel some optimism about the use of wikis in classrooms. Just because a classroom wiki is currently used for low-level purposes does not mean that it will always be used in this way. Wikis and the ways in which they are used have the capacity to evolve. Many of the wikis examined for this chapter were clearly exploratory. They could be read as early forays into making use of new technologies in classroom contexts; attempts to figure out how to use these tools in ways that were useful within the requirements of curriculum and school culture; and recognition that engaging with these practices is a first move towards more meaningful participation. Some of the wikis were actively used to create networks and to distribute information and user-produced content. This in itself is an engagement with aspects of participatory culture. These are important first steps.

## Back to James

This is where James, his text and his piece of writing come back into focus. In his classroom and home, James is learning about the power of a particular form of text and his rights as author. He is being mentored into practices and attitudes around participating in a particular print community that has a long history. This is powerful and important. However, this once dominant technology and knowledge economy now sits alongside technologies and practices that challenge older models of authorship and ownership. The model of childhood that underpins print economies is no longer the only model in operation. As Postman noted more than 25 years ago, shifts in access to information articulate into shifting experiences and views of childhood. For James and his classmates to thrive in this environment, they will need explicit mentoring into the practices associated with new digital texts and the emerging participatory Zeitgeist. They will need to understand and work with information in ways that are appropriate to the time in which they live. Miller (2005) observes that we are experiencing a 'transition from the view of writing as a product to the understanding of writing and reading as moments in a process of communication. In our terms, we no longer say we "are" authors. Instead we periodically author, read, and share information' (p. 40). This is an important distinction.

James and his classmates need to engage with the types of issues brought to the fore in critiques and analyses of *Wikipedia*. James needs to develop the awareness that fact and knowledge are contingent, that texts are increasingly multimodal and fluid, that the identifiable 'author' of print culture is not always at the centre of text production, that not all information is the same, that texts of different types are produced in a range of different communities and that knowledge and expertise can be distributed across a network. He needs to be able to use an array of textual resources and a range of different media, online and offline, to participate in ways that have meaning and that bring him positive outcomes. Classroom wikis provide an opportunity for this to take place. Their affordances set a frame in which all children, working with educators, have opportunities to engage with participatory culture in ways that are explicitly explained, mentored and scaffolded. Importantly, this modelling and explication is most pressing for those students who do not have ways to engage with participatory culture in their out-of-school communities. Notions of participatory culture are also associated with issues of equity and access. Jenkins (2006) argues that 'not all participants are created equal. Corporations – and often individuals within corporate media – still exert greater power than any individual consumer or even the aggregate of consumers. And some consumers have greater abilities to participate in this emerging culture than others' (p. 2). For many students, the classroom is their best opportunity for developing literate practices that have value in the broader community. Yet if James and his classroom colleagues only develop print-based skills, with an understanding of their rights and responsibilities around print text, they are being mentored into aptitudes and attitudes that are declining in value in new workplaces and across new social and political formations.

James will always have opportunities to be an 'author'. The emergence of digital technologies and digital texts has not meant the death of the author; rather it has widened the types of practices and types of texts with which the young must engage. James now has needs around textual practice that extend beyond mastery of print and the concepts of authorship, expertise and information attached to print literacy. As educators we need to understand his needs and find ways to address them in our classroom. As I have argued in this chapter, wikis are a good place to start.

## Notes

i  James is a fictional character, based on observations and classroom participation.
ii  Over a period of two days in January 2008, Google searches were used to identify and categorize 50 elementary and middle years/junior high classroom based wikis in the USA and the UK.

## References

Anderson, C. (2007) *The Wikipedia Story*. Accessed 12 August 2008, from www.bbc.co.uk/radio4/factual/pip/psiwo/).

Aries, P. (1962) *Centuries of Childhood*. London: Cape.

Buckingham, D. (2000) *After the Death of Childhood: Growing up in the Age of Electronic Media*. Cambridge: Polity.

Carrington, V. (2005) 'New textual landscapes, information, new childhood', in J. Marsh (ed.), *Popular Culture: Media and Digital Literacies in Early Childhood*. London: Sage. pp. 13–27.

Cover, R. (2004) 'New media theory: electronic games, democracy and reconfiguring the author–audience relationships', *Social Semiotics*, 14(2): 173–91.

Darnton, R. (1988) 'L'Encyclopédie; an eighteenth-century best seller – Diderot's Encyclopédie', *UNESCO Courier*, July. Accessed 12 August 2008, from http://findarticles.com/p/articles/mi_m1310/is_1988_July/ai_6622804

Foucault, M. (1977) 'What is an author?', in M. Foucault, *Language, Counter-Memory, Practice*. Ed. D. Bouchard. Ithaca, NY: Cornell University Press. pp. 113–38.

Frean, A. (2008) 'White bread for young minds, says university professor', *Times Online*, 14 January 2008. Accessed 3 February 2008, from http://technology.timesonline.co.uk/tol/news/tech_and_web/the_web/article3182091.ece

Graham, K.L. (2008) 'Teachers are digikids too: the digital histories and digital lives of young teachers in English primary schools', *Literacy*, 42(1): 10–18.

Jantzen, G. (2001) 'Flourishing: towards an ethic of natality', *Feminist Theory*, 2: 219–32.

Jenkins, H. (2006) *Convergence Culture: Where Old and New Media Collide*. New York: New York University Press.

Jenkins, H., Clinton, K., Purushotma, R., Robison, A. and Weigel, M. (2006) *Confronting the Challenges of Participatory Culture: Media Education for the 21st Century*. Chicago, IL: John D. and Catherine T. MacArthur Foundation.

Jenkins, P. (1992) *Intimate Enemies: Moral Panics in Contemporary Great Britain*. New York: Aldine de Gruyter.

Leuf, B. and Cunningham, W. (2001) *The Wiki Way: Quick Collaboration on the Web*. Upper Saddle River, NJ: Addison Wesley.

McLuhan, M. (1962) *The Gutenberg Galaxy: The Making of Typographic Man*. Toronto: University of Toronto Press.

Miller, N. (2005) 'Wikipedia and the disappearing "author"', *ETC*, January: 37–40.

Postman, N. (1982) T*he Disappearance of Childhood*. New York: Delacorte.

Postman, N. (1994) *The Disappearance of Childhood*. Revised edn. New York: Vintage.

Steinberg, S. and Kincheloe, J. (eds) (1997) *Kinderculture: The Corporate Construction of Childhood*. Boulder, CO: Westview.

Tapscott, D. (1998) *Growing up Digital: The Rise of the New Generation*. New York: McGraw-Hill.

Wilkinson, D. and Huberman, B. (2007) 'Assessing the value of cooperation in Wikipedia', *First Monday*, 12(4). Accessed 12 August 2008, from www.firstmonday.org/issues/issue12_4/wilkinson/

# Download

## Key points

1. Digital texts are frequently multimodal and thus readers need to be. New technologies are providing new ways of making text.
2. These new texts do not always share the same view of the author, information, authority and expertise that underpin traditional printed texts.
3. Wikipedia shows us that some of the ways in which the importance of the author, who gets to create knowledge and who is allowed to claim expertise, have changed.

## In your classroom

1. With your class, undertake an investigation of Wikipedia.
   (a) Look at what it does and doesn't do; debate whether or not it's a good idea to allow non-experts to make encyclopedia entries.
   (b) Discuss the nature of 'fact' and 'knowledge'.
   (c) Do a case study of a Wikipedia entry. Look at the edit logs, do some additional research on the topic, compare and contrast the Wikipedia entry with a traditional, print encyclopedia entry.
2. Create a classroom wiki; experiment and play.
3. Support your students to create wikis around specific projects designed to require collaboration. Remember, wikis do not have to be permanent.
4. Contact schools and classrooms with wikis in other countries; use the wiki as an avenue for expanding your classroom beyond its physical location.

## Further reading

Graham, L. (2008) 'Teachers are digikids too: the digital histories and digital lives of young teachers in English primary schools', *Literacy*, 42(1): 10–18.

Cover, R. (2004) 'New media theory: electronic games, democracy and reconfiguring the author–audience relationships', *Social Semiotics*, 14(2): 173–91.

Lankshear, C. and Knobel, M. (2007) *New Literacies: Everyday Practices and Classroom Learning*. 2nd edn. Maidenhead: Open University Press.

Wenger, E. (1998) *Communities of Practice: Learning, Meaning and Identity*. Cambridge: Cambridge University Press.

# 5

# Negotiating the Blogosphere: Educational Possibilites

*Julia Davies and Guy Merchant*

## Prologue

It is a rainy November evening and a group of English teachers and Further Education (post-16) lecturers, are talking about Web 2.0 as a way of motivating disengaged learners. Julia is leading the discussion and provides examples of blogs produced by people outside of formal education. She shows a blog kept by a young Iraqi woman, *Riverbend*, who reflects on life in Baghdad and gives her viewpoint, in English, on her everyday life as a civilian in a war zone. Another example is a blog kept by a young female American soldier based in Iraq; she speaks of missing her family, of life in the base and of her reading. The contrasts and similarities are poignant and exemplify blogs as 'citizenship journalism' offering different grass-roots perspectives on global politics. However, the teachers are worried and unconvinced. They do not wish to use material that is unverified, suspect and unedited. These web pages may be 'spoofs; just all lies. How do we know?' one asked.

The cautiousness of these teachers is understandable; the time they spend with pupils in class is limited and they need to be confident about materials they introduce and to understand these texts and their context. They do not want to mislead pupils and do want to provide educational experiences that are trustworthy and robust. While talking about these issues later, we, the authors, evaluated how it was that Julia had come to trust these particular blogs and had chosen them as good examples. We realized that Julia had gone through a process of evaluation over time and had learned about the blogs and the bloggers by unconsciously applying a range of different critical literacy strategies to verify their authenticity. For example, she had followed these blogs over a period of time and seen posts that told of events reported elsewhere; the events described were verified by others. The blogs linked to posts on other blogs that dovetailed with their own. The soldier linked to another site – a photosite where images of her, her family and her comrades could be seen – and developed her blog in 'real time' and reflected festivals like Christmas and Easter and so on. We began to realize what we had learned intuitively: that we read carefully not just within the blogs but across texts, exploring their online contexts and understanding them as part of wider networks (Davies and Merchant, 2007). We now realize that to read online texts in a critical way, one needs to see them as more than free-standing, isolated constructs to be deciphered in the same way as paper-based texts (Penrod, 2007; Richardson, 2006). Blogs need to be read and understood as part of a whole wider network of texts whose process of publishing makes a difference to the way they mean and the role they play in society (Lankshear and Knobel, 2006a). This, we have realized, is something we understand because we have participated in the blogging process ourselves. Just as with reading and understanding other types of text, blog reading is a process that can be better understood through participation in online text production, as well as through reading widely across the online context.

By foregrounding this example, we wish to emphasize the importance for educators to participate in a range of online text making practices if they intend to use them as part of their classroom repertoire. It is not enough to know how to set up a blog and how to read and write; there is a need to understand what blogging is, what it can do and how blogs work as part of meaning-making. This involves understanding the conventions and social practices of the blogosphere, as we outline below.

## The social context

In this section we take a step back to think about popular perceptions of blogs and how these impact on the ways in which we see blogging as a literacy practice, in order to argue that blogging is not only suitable for use in schools, but also highly desirable. In the recent past, headline news reports have been preoccupied with the dangers faced by young people who become immersed in online activities (Britten and Saville, 2008). Reports about paedophiles who 'groom' young people online have been particularly lascivious (Schofield, 2005); online bullying through instant messaging systems have led to some headteachers banning the use of this kind of software, even for after school use (*BBC News*, 2007); and there have even been claims that some social networking sites have led to mass suicide bids (Britten and Saville, 2008). The moral panic around children and young people's use of online communication constitutes a general feeling of unease about the rise of a vulnerable and unruly generation of 'techno-subjects' who engage in practices that are unfamiliar to many adults (Luke and Luke, 2001).

The moral panic about new communicative practices does not bode well for the teacher wishing to work with online text production in her classroom. However, it is partly due to online safety concerns (and the need to teach about critical reading) that we believe educators *should* bring these texts into the class-room. While it may be the case that many youngsters are highly adept at producing all kinds of sophisticated texts out of school, it remains the case that many need support in negotiating their way through the social mazes and dilemmas they face. Moreover, there are many who are uninvolved and who are likely to miss out if they are not shown how to become involved in digital text production at school. We argue that a well-informed and experienced literacy teacher is ideally placed to help all pupils read all texts in a critical way. Critical reading will help pupils to explore the meanings and nuances of online texts and it will also make them safer and more responsible participants in our networked society.

## Literacy as a social practice

Drawing on what has become known as the 'New Literacy Studies', we have come to view literacy in a plural sense. We see that there are many types of literacy that arise out of different social contexts and have different values in those different contexts. We therefore believe it is useful for teachers to accommodate this notion of multiple literacies and to understand texts as constructed differently when literacy is used to perform different functions in our everyday lives. We therefore see digital literacy as a set of social practices that are interwoven with contemporary 'ways of being'. In an overview of the New Literacy Studies, Barton (2001, p. 100) suggests that 'nearly all everyday activities in the contemporary world are mediated by literacy and that people act within a textually mediated social world'. An increasing number of these everyday activities are now mediated through online interaction.

In thinking about texts and their social meanings we see online texts, particularly those produced within social networking sites like blogs, as strong examples of 'literacy as a social practice'. The social affordances of these online texts allow us to thicken existing social ties as well as to extend our social networks. This means that there are aspects of online texts that are in some ways unique and reward particular attention in the literacy classroom. As we have seen, the texts need to be understood in terms of their dynamic relationship with related texts, as well as in terms of the way they might represent identities online. We believe these properties can be harnessed to engage and motivate learners.

In this chapter we introduce the idea of blogging in the classroom, since we believe that the software is easy to use, that the templates are 'user friendly' and simple to adapt, and that teachers will be able to quickly learn how to produce them without the need for too much prior technological knowledge. Further, we go on to show how blogs can be used to engage learners in text-making, both as a way of beginning to understand what it means to participate in social networking, and as a way of involving young people in publishing for wider audiences and for a range of purposes.

# What is a blog?

A 'weblog' or 'blog' is one of the most well-established and well-known kinds of social software, and is simply a website that an owner or 'blogger' can update on a regular basis. The word blog is derived from 'weblog'; quite literally a log or record of information presented as a date-ordered template, or as Walker (2003, p. 1) describes it, 'a frequently updated website consisting of dated entries in reverse chronological order'. These entries (or posts) are usually titled, with the most recent posting at the top of the screen. The enormous variety of blogs – sometimes referred to as the 'blogosphere' – includes serious and trivial material and is a largely unregulated clamour of individual and group voices. Depending on one's point of view, this can be seen as a fascinating diversity of human expression or a confusion of unfiltered information and opinion.

It is not so much semantic content that characterizes blogs, but their textual layout that allow us to categorize them as a type. Blogs are formatted, by default, in a reverse chronological order and typically contain sidebars with links and a clear title across the top. While blogs have some of the organizational features of a diary, it would be inaccurate to describe them as an 'online journal'. Admittedly many bloggers (such as Jill Walker) use their blogs in this kind of way – as diaries – but a significantly larger group take advantage of the affordances of the blog for a variety of different purposes. These and many other blogs sit alongside the published ideas, views and interests of lesser known individuals and groups.

# Who's blogging?

Studies of the blogosphere include Mortensen and Walker (2002), our own study of academic blogging (Davies and Merchant, 2007), Lankshear and Knobel's (2006b) typology of blogs and Carrington's (2008) analysis of young people's blogging practices. Mortensen and Walker provide a discussion of what a blog is, what it means to be a blogger and the research potential of blogs. Our study looks at the ways in which academic bloggers perform their professional identities within quite specific communities of practice (Wenger, 1998). Lankshear and Knobel's typology provides a broad description of the diverse social purposes reflected in the blogosphere. They identify 15 different kinds of blog and note that they are an unstable form because they continue to mutate and hybridize. Carrington's study explores the contrasts between young people's everyday blogging practices, against the backdrop of media discourses of risk. These descriptive and analytical studies reflect some of the key themes in research on blogging. They also report on the wider *use* of blogs across the internet, providing theoretical accounts and understandings of blogging as a social practice and a new kind of literacy.

Many novice bloggers set up and abandon blogs without ever adding to their first post, and seasoned bloggers may own several blogs, some of which they maintain and some of which they do not. It is difficult to know whether to count all such blogs as 'live', as well as to ascertain whether a blog has been truly abandoned or not. Actually determining the demographics of those who use blogging software is a task further complicated by difficulties in reported use as opposed to actual active use, and problems identifying whom users actually are. To say that there are more than 70 million live blogs (Sifry, 2007) or 30 million people on Facebook (Zuckerberg, 2007) only provides us with a very crude snapshot. This makes it problematic to assume that young people are equally and actively engaged in social networking activities. To assume, as some have done, that all young people are 'digital natives' (Prensky, 2001) may be inaccurate. Young people come to classrooms with a range of digital technology experiences, and just as we seek to build on other types of knowledge skills and experience, so too the literacy practitioner needs to understand what learners bring, and do not bring, to the classroom. It is important not to make assumptions about learners in this sphere as in any others. We believe that social networking has pervaded our society enough to merit a place in the literacy curriculum; for those with no experience of this kind of activity, we need to provide it, and for those who have experience, we need to develop it.

## The format of blogs

As we mentioned above, trying to characterize blogs is best done in terms of their format rather than their semantic content. Although there are variations in format, blogs share a range of common features that make them quite easily recognizable as blogs.

A blog contains certain standard textual features that tend to 'frame' the changing text that accumulates as the blogger adds to their postings. Typically, blogs will have a title running across the top of the screen; sometimes this will also show the software used (such as Blogger, Wordpress, Xanga, and so on). To either side marginal space is provided to show links, pictures, details about the blogger, and so on.

The date-stamped post in the centre of the blog is used for regular updates. This could simply be a written entry (with or without hyperlinks), or might incorporate other modalities. In Figure 5.1, we illustrate the use of an embedded object – a YouTube video of an Australian television programme – with a written commentary from the blogger. Embedding an item from another online space is a popular feature on many blogs and exemplifies the closely interwoven nature of online texts. This gives a blog a multimodal texture that can draw from a variety of sources. Underneath the date posted entry, most blogs have a 'Comments' feature enabled, which allows readers to interact with the writers by leaving permanent messages that can be read by everyone. Sometimes comments become a substantive feature of a blog – such as on the *Guardian* newsblog (http://blogs.guardian.co.uk/news/) – while on other blogs the comments feature may have been disabled, according to the blogger's preference. Another key feature of most blogs is the 'blogroll'. The blogroll displays and links to sites chosen by the blogger. This is a 'public display of connection' (Danath and Boyd, 2004), which helps characterize the type of blog this is. In this manner, one blog can act as a gateway to an affinity space (Gee, 2004), because of the way readers can trace paths of interest through the hyperlinks. SparcOz (2008) in Figure 5.1, displays his knowledge of others' thinking in the field of information and communications technology (ICT) and education – the subject of his blog – by providing useful links to their work. Furthermore, he has started categorizing (or tagging) his posts; these tags are displayed in the sidebar. Each of these tags, like key words, link to one or more of his posts and allow readers to sift through the material and be selective about what they read.

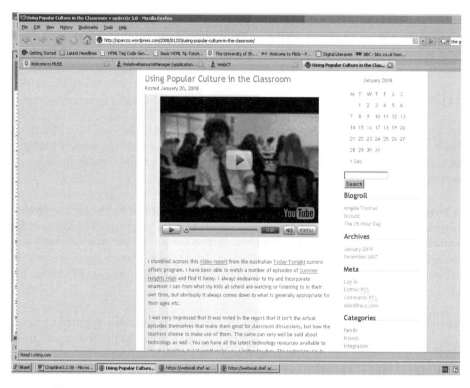

**Figure 5.1** SparcOz teacher blog

Other add-ons or 'widgets' (such as calendars, bookshelves, and slide shows of photographs) involve a simple process of cutting and pasting in order to add them to a blog site. In this way a blogger can personalize his or her own blog, creating a space that can easily look like a professionally produced site. The more bloggers become aware of other social networking sites, the easier it becomes to embed features and add textual materials to their blog. This is an attractive option, since bloggers can quickly populate their blog with tools and links, and in turn, social networking sites become ever more popular online spaces.

Other blogs use a whole range of ways to establish links. Lankshear and Knobel's *Everyday Literacies* (2007) blog (see Figure 5.2) is one example. This blog, jointly authored by two literacy academics, allows them to communicate with other academics and students about their research as they are doing it. Not just within their posts, but also in the sidebar links, they share information about events and activities within the academic community. The 'about me' section allows readers to access links to other blogs the authors are affiliated with and gives information about the aims of the blog. The bloggers show images of their latest books and provide links to the texts and drafts, as well as links to an archive of their academic papers. Hyperlinks within the posts themselves allow the bloggers to 'point' to the organizations they refer to in their text and to literally embed one text within another so that information is quickly shared. The boundaries between and across texts thus become blurred. Hyperlinking in this way also allows the reader some choices – whether to follow references up or not – and different readers will follow different reading paths (Kress, 2003).

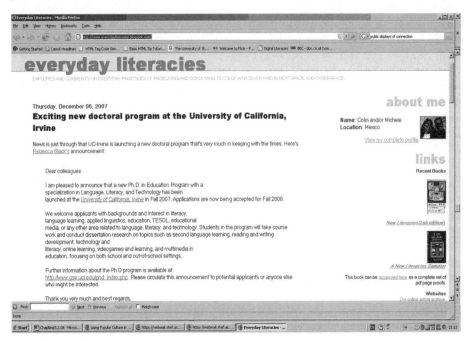

**Figure 5.2** Everday Literacies – an academic blog

Postings can be of whatever length the writer wishes, although short, well written, and concise posts are more likely to be read to the end and may attract more commenters (the life blood of many blogs). It seems that for many blog-gers, comments keep them going; an awareness of audience inspires them to write more. This is, of course, something many teachers are already aware of; a genuine and interested audience is more likely to inspire and engage writers (Penrod, 2007; Richardson, 2006).

## Blogs as a learning tool

As we have seen from our initial exploration, the blog format offers a range of interactive and collaborative possibilities for individuals and groups. Some of these possibilities derive from features that are part of the architecture of blogs. For example, it is easy to set up a blog which allows many to register and post, or for one person to operate a great number of blogs through the same account or user name. But it must also be recognized that during the last five years, a period in which the blogosphere has undergone a rapid expansion, diversifica-tion and innovation have been of central importance.

The sequential and chronological characteristics of the blog format suggest how it can be useful in capturing such things as the development of a narrative, the design and implementation of a project, the progress of research, emerging processes, the aggregation of links or references, and observations or reflections which develop over time. As we saw in the example of SparcOz, blogs are multimodal texts. Written text, still and moving images, or audio content can be used when composing posts, and it is not surprising that some of the most interesting blogs use a judicious combination of these modes. Educational blogging can capture learning as it unfolds over time and this has obvious benefits for both learners and teachers. In this most basic sense, a blog can provide an analytical record of learning, or an online learning journal (Boud, 2001).

Writing in 2003, Efimova and Fielder (2004) noted that, alongside the 'diary-like format' blogs kept for family and friends, there was a 'growing cluster of weblogs used by professionals as personal knowledge repositories, learning journals or networking instruments' (p. 1). They go on to suggest that these newer blogs not only serve the needs and interests of those writing them, but also display emerging ideas in a public space. This suggests the development of more open learning journals that can be interlinked and commented upon within an emerging community of learners.

Richardson (2006) points out that blogging can also involve users in an important and distinctive kind of learning, which he characterizes as 'read-write-think-and-link'. Here he suggests that a blogger develops a kind of practice he calls 'connective writing', in which active reading and involvement through comments and hyperlinks combines with regular posting to support the co-construction of meaning. This view accentuates the significance of a community of bloggers, either in the form of a cluster of related blogs or a group blog. From this point of view we can see blogging as a way of supporting a community of practice (Wenger, 1998) or an affinity space (Gee, 2004). These sorts of networks, as we illustrate below, can be created in and between classrooms through the use of blogs that are connected to each other and to other types of online space. Blogs, in and of themselves, do not necessarily promote social participation, because it is possible to use blogging software without using any hypertextual features. However, we believe that the social and technical affordances of blogs can be beneficially exploited for learning.

In the vignettes below, we illustrate how teachers have shaped the blogging task to allow particular types of learning to take place. In each case the blog produced matches the differing objectives of the teaching sequence by utilizing appropriate technologies at strategic points during the development of the scheme of work that the teacher is following.

## Vignette 5.1: Blogging river pollution

Miss Gupta's class of ten-year-olds is investigating river pollution as part of the Geography curriculum. She has organized the class into mixed-ability teams, each of which will keep a blog. The initial posts are used for statements of what each team thinks about pollution and the environment. After she has taught them how to insert hyperlinks, they are encouraged to search and evaluate web-based sources, recording and commenting on these in their posts. Later, on a field visit, they take digital photographs of environmental hazards such as fly-tipping, invasive non-native flora, industrial effluent, and so on, and then upload them on to their blogs. Towards the end of the unit of work, pupils are asked to reflect on what they have learnt. Miss Gupta sends a letter home with the blog addresses inviting parents to visit and comment if they wish.

In this first vignette, the teacher has considered a number of ways in which blogging can enhance the learning she has planned. Early in the project, blog teams used the medium to express personal opinions and to get feedback comments from their peers. This reflects 'real-world' everyday blogging practice, albeit under the direct guidance of the teacher. She encouraged her pupils to use their blogs as a repository of hyperlinked information and as a document of the class field trip, which helped pupils to explore the visual affordances of blogging. The blogs had a reflective quality, and they were viewed by internet-based parents. These blogs provided a context for collaborative work both within and between the teams. However, they did not attempt to create opportunities for wider social networking beyond the class; such networking was not within the scope of this particular project. This was the teacher's first experience of blogging, and by keeping control of who could comment she could feel more confident because she could control the level of interactivity of the children's blogging practices. Parents' enthusiasm about the project led to requests to open out the commenting facilities further. This demonstrated a new way for parents to become involved in their children's education and reflected further how parents saw the potential of wider publication of their children's writing.

---

## Vignette 5.2: Action adventure blogging

Students at a village primary school in the north of England established a partnership with a similar-aged class about a hundred miles away. The two schools used class blogs to exchange and comment on each others' views and opinions. The work began with posts about favourite films (and tie-in video games such as *The Golden Compass*) and then became more focused as the students discussed action sequences and favourite characters. They later began to post plans of their own stories. When the stories had been written the students made short video trailers which were posted on the blogs. Requests for the full stories were made in blog comments. The stories were then exchanged by email and review posts were displayed on class blogs.

---

The form of blogging described in Vignette 5.2 was explicitly intended to create new connections between students across two schools. This peer networking depended upon, and further developed, collaboration between the teachers so that there were additional professional benefits too. The project involved pupils blogging about the action-adventure genre using film, comic and book sources. This work required careful scheduling so that each teacher was aware when it would be appropriate for pupils to comment on new work as the project progressed, as well as making sure that each class kept in step with the other in terms of curriculum content. In this project, evaluative comment and feedback were key to its success and background work on appropriate ways of doing this provided an important support. Pupils were excited to see fresh postings and new material, and were delighted to share curriculum content and ideas with each other. The *Action Adventure* blogging relates to 'real-world' practices and students were able to use popular blogs such as *Bill's Movie Reviews* (http://billsaysthis.com/movies) and *its very Movie Review* (http://moviereviewblog.net) for ideas.

Both of these examples show how classroom projects can use the affordances of blogs to support learning. The second example also shows how teachers could benefit from the experience as well. Although the blogs concerned had the potential to attract a wider readership, they were designed to serve quite specific and time-limited purposes. Other instances such as photo-blogs have been used to chronicle the progress of a new school building, or to chart the fortunes, fixtures and fitness of the school football team, and have a longer shelf-life, while maybe attracting a more varied readership. Nevertheless the vignettes presented here show authentic blogging practices (that is to say, blogging that reflects everyday or 'real-world' uses of blogs) that are carefully inter-woven with classroom learning.

## Blogging for teachers and pupils

In our work with teachers using blogs in an educational context, we have watched them taking tentative first steps, sensibly aware of the contentious nature of connectivity and keen to ensure pupil safety. They have often taken care to protect pupil identities and have not encouraged pupils to leave comments on blogs outside their own projects. Some teachers are beginning to see how blogging can transform learning in their classroom by providing connections to learners in other contexts, experts in different settings, and to their own families and communities.

While many teachers are keen to use new technologies in their classroom, they often do not exploit the connectivity potential of online spaces. We argue that, ideally, as their confidence and expertise increase, teachers will recognize the real value of using the networking affordances offered by connectivity beyond the classroom. Such experiences with the broader blogosphere will allow learners, under the guidance of teachers, to explore the internet in safe ways and to learn to read and critically interact with the vast amount of text now available online.

Duffy and Bruns (2006) argue that both teachers and learners need to keep up with new developments in digital communication: 'the uses of these technologies – and the technologies themselves – are still developing rapidly, and teachers as well as learners need to keep track of new tools and approaches emerging both in the wider internet community and specifically in educational contexts' (p. 37). Blogs are now a well-established and widely recognized form of digital communication, and this alone suggests that they should be taken seriously in educational settings. As we have argued, the software is easy to use and can be particularly motivating for learners. In blogging projects, children and older students can learn about, and gain first-hand experience of, new literacies. They can learn how to use the affordances of different semiotic modes to make meaning, how to hyperlink their text to others, and get a sense of what online participation is actually like through commenting, and responding to comments, on their own and other people's blogs. We have also argued that the blog format offers new and different ways of capturing and presenting learning in a purposeful way. And, for the more adventurous, the blogosphere can transform pedagogy by opening up classroom learning to a wider and more dispersed audience.

## References

Barton, D. (2001) 'Directions for literacy research: analysing language and social practices in a textually mediated world', *Language and Education*, 15(2/3): 92–104.

*BBC News* (2007) 'Fight cyberbullies, schools told'. 21 September. Retrieved 1 February, from http://news.bbc.co.uk/go/pr/fr/-/1/hi/education/7005389.stm

Boud, D. (2001) 'Using journal writing to enhance reflective practice', in L.M. English and M.A. Gillen (eds), *Promoting Journal Writing in Adult Education: New Directions in Adult and Continuing Education.* San Francisco, CA: Jossey Bass. pp. 9–18.

Britten, N. and Saville, P. (2008) 'Police fear internet cult inspires teen suicides', *Daily Telegraph.* Retrieved 1 February 2008, from www.telegraph.co.uk/news/main.jhtml?xml=/news/2008/01/23/nsuicide123.xml.

Carrington, V. (2008) '"I'm Dylan and I'm not going to say my last name": some thoughts on childhood, text and new technologies', in *British Educational Research Journal*, 34(2): 151–66.

Danath, J. and Boyd, D. (2004) 'Public displays of connection', *BT Technology Journal*, 22(4): 71–82.

Davies, J. and Merchant, G. (2007) 'Looking from the inside out – academic blogging as new literacy', in M. Knobel (ed.), *The New Literacies Sampler.* New York: Peter Lang. pp. 167–97.

Duffy, P. and Bruns, A. (2006) 'The use of blogs, wikis and RSS in education: a conversation of possibilities' [electronic version], *Proceedings Online Learning and Teaching Conference 2006.* Brisbane: QUT. pp. 31–8. Retrieved 4 January 2008, from http://eprints.qut.edu.au/archive/00005398/01/5398.pdf

Efimova, L. and Fiedler, S. (2004) *Learning Webs: Learning in Weblog Networks.* Retrieved 4 January 2008, from http://blog.mathemagenic.com/2003/11/20.html#a844

Gee, J.P. (2004) *What Videogames Have to Teach Us about Learning and Literacy.* New York: Palgrave Macmillan.

Kress, G. (2003) *Literacy in the New Media Age.* London: Routledge.

Lankshear, C. and Knobel, M. (2006a) *New Literacies: Everyday Practices and Classroom Learning.* 2nd edn. Maidenhead: Open University Press.

Lankshear, C. and Knobel, M. (2006b) 'Weblog worlds and constructions of effective and powerful writing: cross with care, and only where signs permit', in K. Pahl and J. Rowsell (eds), *Travel Notes from the New Literacy Studies; Instances of Practice.* Clevedon: Multilingual Matters. pp. 72–92.

Lankshear, C. and Knobel, M. (2007) *Everyday Literacies.* Retrieved 1 February 2008, from http://everydayliteracies.blogspot.com/

Luke, A. and Luke, C. (2001) 'Adolescence lost/childhood regained: on early interventions and the emergence of the techno-subject', *Journal of Early Childhood Literacy*, 1(1): 91–120.

Mortensen, T. and Walker, J. (2002) 'Blogging thoughts: personal publication as online research tool', in A. Morrison (ed.), *Researching ICTs in Context.* Oslo: Intermedia Report. pp. 249–79.

Penrod, D. (2007) *Using Blogs to Enhance Literacy.* Lanham, MD: Rowman and Littlefield.

Prensky, M. (2001) *Digital Game-based Learning.* New York: McGraw-Hill.

Richardson, W. (2006) *Blogs, Wikis, Podcasts and Other Powerful Webtools for Classrooms.* Thousand Oaks, CA: Corwin Press.

Schofield, J. (2005) 'Blogging "a paedophile's dream"', *Guardian Unlimited: Technology.* Retrieved 1 February 2008, from http://blogs.guardian.co.uk/technology/2005/01/27/blogging_a_paedophiles_dream.html.

SparcOz (2008) *SparcOz 5.0.* Retrieved 1 February 2008, from http://sparcoz.wordpress.com/

Sifry, D. (2007) 'The state of the live Web, April 2007', *Sifry's Alerts.* Retrieved 13 August 2008, from www.sifry.com/alerts/archives/000493.html

Walker, J. (2003) *Weblog Definition.* Retrieved 14 April 2008, from http://jilltxt.net/

archives/blog_theorising/final_version_of_weblog_definition.html.
Wenger, E. (1998) *Communities of Practice: Learning, Meaning and Identity*. Cambridge: Cambridge University Press.
Zuckerberg, M. (2007) 'Facebook founder says social networking sites in it for long haul', *Guardian Unlimited*. Retrieved 18 October 2007, from www.guardian.co.uk/technology/2007/oct/18/

# Download

## Key points

1. Blogs are a good introduction to Web 2.0 software in the classroom because they are free, widely available and easy to use. Teachers can enable and disable different features according to their preference.
2. Blogs allow users to incorporate different modes of communication, for example, by embedding videos, sound files and images, thus introducing pupils to the concept of multimodal communication.
3. Blogs provide the possibility of instant online publication and ongoing networking with others.

## In your classroom

1. Pupils can work in teams on the production of blogs that record project development as it unfolds over time.
2. Pupils can develop critical reading skills by analysing and identifying the defining characteristics and features of blogs. This will also help them to understand the affordances and constraints of blogs and inform their own blogging.
3. Pupils can use blogs to connect with learners in different contexts, such as schools following a similar project in a different location.

## Further reading

Davies, J. and Merchant, G. (2009) *Web 2.0 for Schools: Social Participation and Learning*. New York: Peter Lang.
Knobel, M. and Lankshear, C. (2007) *The New Literacies Sampler*. New York: Peter Lang.
Richardson, W. (2006) *Blogs, Wikis, Podcasts and Other Powerful Web Tools for Classrooms*. Thousand Oaks, CA: Corwin Press.

# Virtual Worlds in Real-life Classrooms

*Guy Merchant*

## Introduction

In the autumn of 2006 planning began on an innovative project, initiated by Barnsley Metropolitan Borough Council (Barnsley MBC), which aimed to raise literacy attainment for boys in the nine to eleven years age range. Arrangements had been put in place to design a 3D virtual world in which pupils would be engaged in purposeful interaction and communication. Literacy would play a key role within the virtual world which would in turn provide a key context for literacy learning. New technology, it was thought, would both stimulate and motivate the pupils.

The idea that digital technology might help to motivate reluctant learners and provide more meaningful contexts for literacy has captured the attention of an increasing number of educators (Merchant, 2007b). In this particular project, some members of the planning team had already been introduced to new thinking about digital literacy (Lankshear and Knobel, 2007) and, in particular, the educational potential of video-gaming (Gee, 2004). Although virtual world gameplay was beyond the experience of most members of the planning team, there was a general sense that it would be a worthwhile development that could enhance provision in local classrooms.

In partnership with the company Virtually Learning (www. virtuallylearning.co.uk), the project team – a group of education consultants and teachers – set to work designing the virtual world that students could explore in avatar-based game-play (Dovey and Kennedy, 2006). On-screen avatars, or computer-generated characters, would be controlled by students using keyboard strokes, thus allowing them to navigate their way around the virtual world. It was proposed that students would work collaboratively to construct their own narratives from

multiple, ambiguous clues seeded in the world and, as a result, would be motivated to engage in both online and offline literacy activities. This led to the
creation of a virtual world called *Barnsborough*, a three-dimensional environment explored on desktop computers from multiple but unique perspectives
through avatars in local Active Worlds browsers (see Figure 6.1). Pupils in ten
different project schools are now able to engage in this sort of virtual world
gameplay, and as they play they can interact through a real-time chat facility
somewhat similar to MSN messenger.

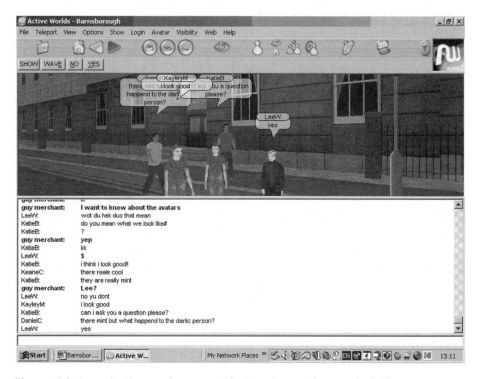

**Figure 6.1** Interviewing students outside Barnsborough town hall (first person
view)

The world itself consists of a number of interconnected zones that are lifelike
and familiar – in fact they are often modelled on real-world objects. The zones
include a town centre, complete with streets, alleyways, cafés, shops and
administrative buildings, some of which can be entered. There is also a park
with a play area, bandstand, boating lake, mansion, woodland and hidden
caves; a residential area with Victorian and contemporary housing; a petrol sta-
tion and various local amenities; and an industrial zone with old factories,
canals, and so on. In some of the connecting zones pupils may encounter other
sites such as a large cemetery, a medieval castle and a stone circle.

Visitors to Barnsborough discover a world littered with evidence of human
activity. Its previous inhabitants have simply vanished, leaving behind traces of

their everyday lives in their notes, posters and journals. Phones are ringing and some have audio or text messages; computers have been left running; alarms are going; and vehicles simply abandoned. Rich media, tool-tip clues, and hyperlinked and downloadable texts provide clues about the previous inhabitants of Barnsborough, suggesting a number of reasons why they have rather hurriedly abandoned the area. Some possible storylines include a major biohazard, alien abduction, a political or big business disaster, or something more mysterious. The planning team has seeded these clues throughout the Barnsborough environment.

The desktop experience creates the illusion of a three-dimensional space in which avatars act as visual representations of users who interact and communicate synchronously (Dickey, 2003). Barnsborough is, in summary, a high-resolution graphic environment that provides a stimulating context for online exploration and interaction. The initial aim of the project was to provide a place to enact loosely structured open-ended and multilayered narratives, although as time moved on, as we shall see, activity has become more consistently anchored to classroom literacy routines. At the time of writing, this virtual world is still being used to enrich the literacy curriculum in Year 5 and Year 6 classes (students from nine to eleven years of age) in Barnsley MBC and provides an environment for:

• collaborative thinking and problem-solving;
• engaging in a variety of themed literacy practices;
• exploring multimedia and multimodal texts; and
• negotiating meanings and values.

Debates about the educational worth of video-gaming and virtual world gameplay have recently attracted considerable attention (see the Byron Review, 2007). Although a considerable amount of popular debate has focused on the possible negative effects of gaming – particularly exposure to inappropriate or violent content – empirical research that investigates their learning potential in classrooms is still in its infancy. At the same time, while claims are made about high levels of learner engagement in video-gaming (Squires, 2002) and the potential to design powerful learning environments using virtual world technology (Dede et al., 2006), there is clearly scope for more evidence to support these claims. Some researchers have in fact suggested that these immersive environments may lead to loss of focus and distraction (Lim et al., 2006), but the evidence is insufficient to reach any firm conclusions. Earlier studies, such as those conducted by Ingram et al. (2000) focused on the complexity of virtual world chat, giving weight to the argument that the written conversations that take place are an emerging and important form of synchronous interaction – a new kind of literacy.

The work of the Vertex Project (Bailey and Moar, 2001), which involved primary school students in the UK, most closely matches the Barnsborough initiative. Although the Vertex Project report makes some interesting observations on avatar gameplay, it placed much greater emphasis on building and creating virtual world content than the work described here, which centres on digital literacy (Merchant, 2007a). Nevertheless, a common theme that unites these studies is the need for careful consideration of how to integrate these new ways of learning into classroom contexts. As Squires (2002, p. 10) argues, 'the educational value of the game-playing comes not from the game itself, but from the creative coupling of educational media with effective pedagogy to engage students in meaningful practices'. This observation on gameplaying could also be applied to the use of 3D virtual worlds, where the kinds of interaction promoted and the immersive nature of the experience contrast with conventional classroom routines. The question of how teachers use virtual world technology for educational purposes, and indeed the role that they themselves adopt in virtual world gameplay, emerges as a key theme in this work. This theme is explored in more detail below.

## Researching the virtual world

Literature on research methodology in the social sciences is frequently concerned with philosophical questions concerning the 'reality' of a particular situation and the relative significance of the meanings or interpretations of the various actors and researchers involved (Denzin and Lincoln, 2003). When part of the reality of a situation is virtual, and the actors and researchers are both physically embodied and actualized in the virtual world as avatars, the research context can be conceived as a number of layered realities.

When researching a virtual world like Barnsborough, it is necessary to understand the architecture of the environment itself as a complex 3D multimodal text; a reality that has been constructed by the planners and designers. It is also necessary, however, to make sense of how meanings are subsequently made by the teachers and students involved, as well as their avatars that populate the world. Teachers and students in this project inhabit a number of interrelated 'realities'. These include the realities of conventional literacy and information and communications technology (ICT) lessons, as well as their experiences of being in the virtual world (itself another sort of reality). Researching the perspectives and understandings of teachers and students means looking at these different realities and attempting to read them in relation to one another, and being able to account for other key influences such as popular culture and prior gameplay experience.

Observing interaction in the virtual world – an obvious starting point – is problematic in a number of ways. First, in order to actually see interaction in context, one needs to be part of that context and that involves a level of participation. As researcher, I have to enter the virtual world as an avatar, others rapidly perceived my presence, and I quickly become part of the flow of events taking place. In other words, I disrupt the very nature of the interactions I seek to observe. In this way, a very familiar research dilemma is reproduced in the virtual world. The researcher begins to change the reality that she or he is try-ing to interpret (Rosaldo, 1989).

However, another option is available to the researcher. With administrator rights, one can become invisible and hide round corners, behind walls, under the ground, and so on. Other avatars will normally be unaware of one's exis-tence. Working this way was a strange experience. The thrill of espionage quickly gave way to the uncomfortable feeling of being a voyeur, eavesdrop-ping on the actions and interactions of others. As an invisible presence watching others while they were blissfully unaware, I had, in a sense, achieved the ultimate non-interventionist state. I could become an 'objective' non-par-ticipant observer, although, of course, I would still have all my beliefs and assumptions and my presence as an avatar – albeit an invisible one! But this ideal-sounding position was simultaneously ethically dubious, emotionally uncomfortable and methodologically questionable. Should we be observing students, or for that matter any human subject, without their informed con-sent? And what about their rights to participate in or withdraw from a particular study? So, instead of using this approach, data on students' interac-tions in the virtual world were collected by classroom observations. Further insights into their experience of working in the world, and using and choosing avatars, were gained through in-world group interviews conducted shortly after observational visits.

This chapter draws on research data from a number of sources. First, participant observation of the planning processes and educational design of Barnsborough were collected in my own field notes. These were supplemented by minutes of meetings and email exchanges. A small set of screenshots of in-world planning meetings was also archived. Secondly, I conducted in-class observations of pupils working in the virtual world, following these up with group interviews conducted in the virtual world. Thirdly, to gain some initial views from partic-ipating teachers I conducted teacher interviews in the virtual world.

## Creating and controlling the virtual world

Planning the virtual world involved a small group comprised of local literacy and drama specialists, ICT advisory staff, primary school teachers, and myself as consultant and researcher. Knowledge and first-hand experience of this sort of environment was minimal. In our initial meeting the concept of exploring a 'computer world with aviators [sic]' was described, as we struggled to find a common language to share what we envisaged. From the start I was interested in how the powerful technology and potential of a virtual world might be har-nessed for educational purposes with young learners, as a logical extension of my ongoing research into digital literacy (Merchant, 2007b). The process of planning the virtual world was carefully tracked in my own field notes and minutes of meetings. In this section I draw mainly from these sources to iden-tify pervasive themes such as the design of the environment, the texts developed, views on risk and appropriateness, and the limitations that were imposed.

## The environment

As Schroeder (2002) observes, designing virtual worlds and the avatars that inhabit them both creates and limits possibilities in terms of places, identities and social lives. Designing such a world simultaneously involves acts of creation and control. In our initial meetings it quickly became clear that there was strong commitment to the idea that the world would actively engage pupils who were sometimes hard to reach, as well as providing motivation to use literacy in a variety of purposeful ways. Our early discussions focused on choosing the right kind of environment, with some of the team arguing for a traditional English village and others favouring a post-industrial urban setting. Other possibilities, including futuristic and historic settings, were quickly discarded as discussion polarized around the competing ideas of rural idyll and urban realism. In the end, we opted for the latter; Barnsborough would have the feel of a slightly run-down modern urban environment with some pockets of prosperity. It would partly reflect pupils' everyday reality, but also incorporate some features more reminiscent of urban videogames. The town's surrounding areas would be suburban and semi-rural in feel. The design team agreed that this environment offered enough possibilities and would also be appealing to pupils in the participating schools.

Although there was some pupil consultation, these and subsequent decisions were predominantly based on what the adult planners *imagined* that students would respond to best. In this sense we were creating a world that we thought students would wish to inhabit. There are interesting parallels here with the ways in which classrooms and other learning environments are constructed. In an educational environment that is dominated by statutory curricula, and the associated discourses of learning objectives and measurable outcomes, it is easy to overlook how often educators' decisions also include views about what will be 'good' for learners in a more general sense, and what they think will capture pupils' interest. These views contribute to the ways in which orderliness and legitimacy are invariably imposed by adults in authority, and reflect the uncomfortable notion that a classroom community has only successfully been created when teachers succeed in establishing a unified social world (Pratt, 1991). This is a theme I shall return to later, because it embodies a set of assumptions that are troubled by new technology and digital literacy.

## Texts for teaching

Having decided upon the environment, the planning group's attention quickly turned to the construction of narrative clues, and particularly to writing content for the tool-tip clues and the hyperlinked and downloadable texts. For the most part, the kinds of texts produced for the world were dictated by our knowledge of the genres referred to in national English policy documents (for example, Primary Framework, 2007), governed as we were by the challenge to raise attainment in literacy. However, other kinds of digital texts, such as text messages, MSN-type chat, and audio and video clips, were also included. One of the participating teachers commented that these were 'new genres' of writing and she was a key influence in establishing this perspective with participating teachers. Nevertheless, in the overarching context of concern to raise standards in literacy, associated most closely with high-stakes testing in print literacy, this project's aim to use new technologies, and to give validity to the digital literacies associated with them (Merchant, 2007a), was a bold move. Perhaps because of this, our ideas were continually being re-framed by participating teachers in terms of what literacy could be taken *out* of the virtual world and used in conventional literacy routines, which sometimes led to an under-valuing of literacy *in* the virtual world.

The comment made by a teacher's avatar in an in-world planning meeting (see Figure 6.2) provides a useful illustration of this tension. The comment implies that online text only becomes educational once it is deployed in the pedagogical routine called 'literacy'. This exposes the tension that exists between the idea of using an immersive and literacy-rich virtual world as a context for incidental but purposeful *uses* of digital literacy and the focus on *teaching* literacy, which was understandably foremost in some of the teachers' minds.

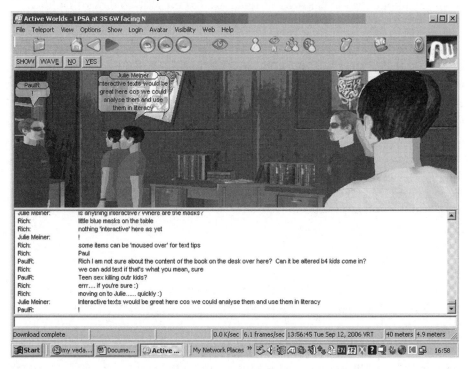

**Figure 6.2** The planning group in Barnsborough town hall (first person view)

## Risk and appropriateness

Notions of appropriateness were quick to surface once the planners began to explore the virtual world for themselves. Occasionally material placed in the world by the Virtually Learning team was seen as unsuitable for the age range. For example, in the meeting captured in the Figure 6.2 screenshot, there was a book on the table with the title *Is Teen Sex Killing Our Kids?* It was removed following the comment 'Can it be altered b4 the kids come in?' This episode reflects an overarching concern with the creation of a safe and secure virtual world; this theme is explored below.

Barnsborough is a heavily protected place. Only ten schools and the planning team have access, but nonetheless, safety is seen as a key issue and regularly surfaces as a topic for conversation. Questions such as 'Are the world-builders police-checked?' and 'What if a teaching assistant, volunteer or parent logged on?' have been asked. The planning team painstakingly made sure that everything was safe enough for the school environment. In addition to this there were concerns about pupil interaction and the potential for bullying, verbal abuse and inappropriate behaviour. The tensions that arose are captured in field notes:

> We're currently wrestling with questions about the supervision/monitoring of children's chat. At the sharp end, these are questions about children's safety and teachers' responsibilities ... but they are pitted against notions of pupil autonomy and teacher control, as well as the wish to provide children with rich experiences of new literacies.

When Barnsborough is fully populated it is possible that up to three hundred users could be online at one time. More probably, it would be two or three classes from different schools. This would still be difficult to monitor, if indeed monitoring is what teachers need to do. This again highlights the issue of the teacher's role, which was interpreted by participants in different ways. In some cases, role was limited to supervision of the classroom environment and of pupils, and pupil interaction in the virtual world. This tended to be consistent with the view that the world provided a playful stimulus for follow-up work in literacy lessons. Other teachers adopted a more didactic role as 'teacher in Barnsborough', suggesting that they saw instructional opportunities as part of the virtual world experience.

## Limitation

As the planning team became more familiar with virtual world gameplay, their own enjoyment of rapid and sometimes chaotic chat, coupled with unrestricted movement and exploration, often created a heady atmosphere. In the current educational climate it is unusual to be part of a planning group that has fun! However, the free-form nature of this gameplay presented a direct challenge to professional sensibilities. Convinced that students would enjoy Barnsborough as much as they were beginning to, the planners began to wonder how they would control a class of youngsters who would undoubtedly be both more dexterous with the controls and more unruly in their behaviour.

Relatively early on in these discussions it was agreed that the avatars' 'fly' function should be disabled for students. It was also agreed that other possibilities such as sending one-to-one telegrams and whispering (private chat) would not be introduced to the students. Other teleporting possibilities now used routinely by the planning team would also be kept 'secret'. And, finally, as we shall see, the town zone of Barnsborough would be sealed off. Students would enter the town through the sewers and would be free to explore the town, but would not be allowed access to other zones. This would help teachers to retain control, and more importantly, to point students in particular directions and to engage them in activities which would tie in to more traditional literacy activities. In a sense, the virtual world was beginning to become more like the real world, with students being guided in their exploration of Barnsborough in a way that often resembled a school outing.

Our perceived responsibility as educators meant that, in the name of safety and professional compliance to a particular discourse about literacy, we created a walled garden: a closed system which would make surveillance easier and learning more controlled. In short we constructed boundaries that could be policed in an attempt to re-create a unified social world (Pratt, 1991).

## Acts of transgression

The very act of taking virtual world gameplay to school clearly raises some important issues for teachers. The whole concept of gameplay, and the notion that students might actually learn in game-like environments, contrasts with dominant interpretations of the curriculum. After all if 'games' are associated with the sequential development of skills in the physical education curriculum, then 'play' is effectively marginalized in many primary schools and in a school day dominated by the formal curriculum. Furthermore, in a contemporary UK school environment, unregulated internet access and online peer-to-peer interaction are certainly not the norm. And so it is not surprising to find that the world of Barnsborough soon began to mirror the world of the classroom and that virtual world activity was often perceived as a stimulus for the real work that would follow. The rule-bound world that began to take shape has been described above, but where there are rules there are also transgressions. In this section I document some of these.

The Barnsborough environment was designed for exploration but, as we saw above, unfettered exploration was seen by the classroom teachers as being too difficult to contain and potentially chaotic. In an attempt to solve these problems Barnsborough town was initially sealed off, so that child avatars could not explore the park area and what lay beyond, and students were asked to restrict their search for clues to the town centre. However, it wasn't long before they discovered that by climbing up on objects they could launch themselves over the wall and land on the other side (freedom) as the gravitational pull of the virtual world brought their avatars back down to ground level. Teachers requested help from Virtually Learning technical staff, who eventually 'dragged' the escaped avatars back to the town. Perhaps these child avatars were making history in becoming the first truants in a virtual world! Here again, the idea of Barnsborough as a place for guided investigation rather than immersive exploration tended to dominate classroom practices.

When designing Barnsborough, the planning team were keen to avoid any suggestions of violence and agreed early on that there should be no weapons in the world. This was also carefully explained to the students involved in the project. Moreover, avatars would not be able to perform any routine aggressive actions (such as karate kicks). At the same time, we recognized that many of the students would draw on their experiences of video-gaming when interacting with the virtual world. We were not altogether surprised, on one occasion, to observe a child avatar excitedly announcing that a gun had been found lying on the ground: 'I tried to pick it up but I couldn't.' In actual fact the child had merely seen a shadow and had mistaken it for a weapon! Arming one's avatar by picking up weapons is, of course, a common feature in video games and it is not surprising to see this strategy applied in a different context. Harmless though this episode was, it illustrates a subtle kind of boundary-crossing transgression because it operates from a different set of rules and assumptions.

In a similar way, some teachers subverted the focused in-world activities that had been generated by members of the planning group. An example of this was the use of the 'hide-and-seek' game, in which one of the avatars would hide and then others would be challenged to locate them. This playful interaction, and the onscreen texts that it generated, was starkly different to some of the more teacher-directed sessions in which the discourse patterning more closely resembled classroom talk. In the following extract we see this at work, with pupils exchanging tips about shortcuts in order to perform the hidden functions of flying and running (T is the teacher):

> KM: GA do you know how to run?
> GA: probely why do u wanna no
> KM: no
> JB: A let's pla hid'n'seek
> KM: its altgr and the up button
> T: Bet you can't find me JB!
> GA: bet i can
> JB: gis sum clus wire yu ar
> MH: JP how do you fy
> JB: f
> JB: f12
> JP: keep tapin it

A final example of transgressive behaviour stems from the use of avatars. Although Barnsborough avatars cannot be customized by users, they have distinctive visual characteristics that mark age, gender and ethnicity. This has led to some interesting interactions, some of which are captured in field notes:

> ... how our avatar looks and dresses attracts attention. I was interested to note yesterday how children working were concerned about the gender of their avatar and offered each other online guidance on how to select a more appropriate one. But not only that, our teachers too were trying on different bodies, checking each other out, rotating etc. – 'how does my bum look in these dungarees?'

## Digital literacy

To enter Barnsborough is to become immersed in a textual universe and to participate in what Steinkuehler (2007, p. 297) has described as a 'constellation of literacy practices'. Below I list the main kinds of digital literacy encountered in the virtual world. These were not directly studied or used for literacy instruction, with the exception of the hyperlinked texts that were quite deliberately tied to literacy objectives in the English Primary National Strategy.

### Environmental signs and notices

This material forms part of the texture of the 3D virtual world and is designed to provide both a real-world feel to the visual environment and clues for students. Examples of this include graffiti, logos, posters and advertisements.

### Tool-tips

These give additional explanations or commentaries on in-world artefacts and are revealed when moused-over with the cursor. Tool-tip messages are shown in text boxes and draw attention to environmental features ('looks like someone's been here'); hold navigational information ('you'll need a code to get in'); or provide detail ('cake from Trinity's').

### Hyperlinked texts

Mouse-clicking on active links reveals a more extended text. Examples include an oil-drilling proposal (Word document), a child's diary (Flash document) and a web page on aliens. Some of these links are multimedia (such as phone messages and music clips) whereas others provide examples of different text types, such as text messages and online chats.

### Interactive chat

This is the principal means of avatar interaction and involves synchronous chat between visitors to the world. This is represented as speech bubbles above the avatars' heads and in scrolling playscript format in the chat window beneath the 3D display (see Figure 6.2).

The inclusion of these features meant that pupils were given an immersive experience of digital literacy. When interviewed, both in the classroom and in-world, the students were vociferous in their enthusiasm for Barnsborough, as the following extract shows:

> JB: its mint i like barnsbrough because its really adventurous its abosulutly brilliand MINTUS!!
> KC: its a mystery
> JM: i like it because u get to exsplor the town
> guy: um
> JB: *brilliant
> guy: what's your favourite place?
> JB: thinternet cafe
> guy: tell me why?
> JB: *internet cafe
> KC: town hall
> JB: i like internet cafe because lots of uknown thing have happened in there
> JM: town hall cause its really big and so is the streets too!
> KC: because its hard to find clues
> guy: clues? what clues?
> JM: leflets also we all think theres alians!
> KC: like the oil drilling proposel
> guy: what's happened here?
> JB: well green triangles they really freak me out and also we have found some gas masks and boyes with poison in them alover barnsbrough also some alien footsteps
> guy: Someone's been up to something!!
> JB: we dont know yet but that is what we are trying to find out BUT i thing barnsbrough has been invaded by aliens

But it is not simply that this virtual experience is 'brilliant', the extract also shows how the students are learning about the conventions of online chat (note JB's correction of her typo 'brilliand' to '*brilliant'). When asked about the chat function they repeatedly described it as 'cool' or suggested that they 'like it a lot', with some students arguing that it helps improve typing speed. Some of the teachers also saw the benefits of this kind of interaction and suggested that students' use of chat had developed over time:

> AC: ... the chat is reading and writing without the children realising. The way the chat has developed over the course of the units has reflected this
> guy: can you say how it has changed?
> AC: Gone from the text/chat language and the 'Hi' to children actually using it as a method of finding things out from each other and discussing issues raised from the world or the work set

More explicit teaching in-world, using the chat function, was undertaken by some of the project schools. This chat data is interesting in the way that it replicates the characteristic features of spoken discourse in classroom settings. In the following extract the teacher has led her class into the park zone. Here there are some formal gardens, a play area with swings and a roundabout. Children also notice the bandstand situated next to the lake (here referred to as the 'poned'). The teacher allows the children to explore – there is a considerable amount of avatar mobility – but also attempts to keep them focused. Trying to imagine 'how the park was' is the explicit aim, which is reinforced at the start of the extract. The pattern of teacher questioning and feedback is quite familiar, as are the moves to keep children on task, such as the response to J's question about avatars. If it were not for the fact that this conversation was digitally mediated it might seem rather unremarkable:

> Teacher: ... remember what the focus of this lesson is! What was the park like before whatever happened happened?
> SS: we think it must have been busy
> Teacher: What makes you think that S?
> CM: mm-there are some cake on the band stand so people must have been eating while playing
> Teacher: Excellent observation C.
> LF: go to the poned jm
> DC: I bet some elders would admire the flowers
> CM: .0
> SS: because it says there is a public meeting in the park
> Teacher: What did you want me to look at/
> JB: why are other people names on avatar
> Teacher: J – you should not be messing with the avatar function. Keep focused on what we are supposed to be doing!

Despite the fact that some teachers saw the immersive online experience as 'literacy by stealth', recognizing how children were engaged in literacy practices through their playful engagement and exploration of the world, it was primarily seen as a stimulus for more traditional literacy work. When speaking of the benefits of the virtual world work, these were usually indexed to improvements in print literacy and related practices such as speaking and listening. Given this emphasis, and the fact that hyperlinked and downloadable texts were cross-referenced to national literacy objectives, traditional literacy skills were privileged. Not surprisingly, this was also quite clear from the students' perspective. They were also well aware that they were 'doing literacy', as this second interview extract reveals:

> SJ: weve done loads of things on barnsborough
> GP: its good real good
> guy: yes GP
> SJ: newspaper repots taking notes flash back story loads!!
> GB: we have been doing notes writing reports and doing a flashback story

This extract is interesting because, when describing what they have done in Barnsborough, the children fall back on a description of 'text types' using the discourse of curriculum literacy. It appears that they have tacitly accepted the teacher model of using the virtual world as a stimulus for classroom literacy, rather than as a literacy experience in and of itself.

## Challenges for teachers

The work undertaken on this virtual world project has raised a number of significant issues. One repeated theme concerns the sort of learning environment we want for children and the extent to which adult views assume a consensual social world with rather arbitrary boundaries. This theme runs through from the original plans to early experimentation in the virtual world. We can see how the potential for new approaches to learning is constrained by professional concern and the more general educational climate in which it is embedded. But digital literacy has a subversive influence because it allows users to see the possibilities for different kinds of teacher–learner relationship, different kinds of learning and interaction, and different genres and purposes for literacy. This subversive potential is also evident in the data.

The work also reflects a wider picture in which powerful and available new technologies, which enable informal learning and social networking, are beginning to disrupt the control traditionally exerted by educators (see Davies and Merchant, 2009). So great is this threat of destabilization that a number of new technologies are currently excluded from educational settings and we continually attempt to police the online activity of our pupils.

Working in a virtual world also brings teachers face to face with some complex and challenging issues. After a number of years of being locked down by a narrow and prescriptive curriculum, constantly operating under the shadow of professional accountability, using online gameplay is a risky business. Teachers and researchers involved in such work must ask themselves some key questions:

- How easy is it to leave the comfort zone of conventional, classroom-based student–teacher relationships and experiment with new and fluid online interactions? Virtual worlds can be unfamiliar and chaotic environments in which conventional routines and control strategies are of little use. Teachers will have to take risks when using this sort of technology, and both teachers and researchers need to document the new ways of working that emerge.
- What are the implications of working in an environment in which some pupils are more experienced or confident than the teacher? As in many other applications of new technology, children tend to be more experienced and more adaptable. Although this is not always the case, teachers do need to be prepared to learn from pupils and to value their experimentation.
- How can this sort of work be justified and defended in an educational environment which regularly lurches back to a preoccupation with 'the basics' and traditional print literacy skills? New and important digital literacies can be introduced through virtual world gameplay. Experience of these is likely to have a positive impact on learning in general and on literacy in whatever form. Again, more evidence is needed to support this case.
- How can the level of immersion and flexible online access required by such work be accommodated within the constraints of current resource and

timetable structures? As others have observed (for example, Holloway and Valentine, 2002) schools need to rethink computer hardware location, access and use. In common with other digital literacy practices, virtual world gameplay invites a more flexible approach to curriculum organization and online access.

- What additional planning and co-ordination work is necessary to make the most of online work as a medium that facilitates exchange between year groups and interaction between schools? One of the most important features of digital literacy is its potential to connect learners with others outside the immediate school environment. This will involve careful co-ordination and planning between teachers in different locations.
- What real or perceived risks may be faced when engaging in virtual world gameplay (for example, child protection, parental censure, and so on)? The Barnsborough project paid rigorous attention to issues of online safety. As well as this, parents were kept informed about the project. We were well aware of the moral panic about gameplay and carefully rehearsed the educational rationale for the work of the project.

The small-scale initiative described here exemplifies how these wider issues are being played out in local circumstances. It also shows that teachers need not be the docile operatives of an outdated, centralized curriculum, but can instead respond innovatively to the learning potential of powerful new technologies.

# References

Bailey, F. and Moar, M. (2001) 'The Vertex Project: children creating and populating 3D virtual worlds', *International Journal of Art and Design Education*, 20(1): 19–30.

Byron Review (2007) *Safer Children in a Digital World: The Final Report of the Byron Review*. Retrieved 20 August 2008, from www.dcsf.gov.uk/byronreview/pdfs/Final%20Report%20Bookmarked.pdf

Davies, J. and Merchant, G. (2009) *Web 2.0 for Schools: Social Participation and Learning*. New York: Peter Lang.

Dede, C., Clarke, J., Ketelhut, D., Nelson, B. and Bowman, C. (2006) 'Fostering motivation, learning and transfer in multi-user virtual environments', paper given at the 2006 American Educational Research Association conference, San Franscisco, CA, April.

Denzin, N.K. and Lincoln,Y.S. (2003) 'The discipline and practice of qualitative research', in N.K. Denzin and Y.S. Lincoln (eds), *The Landscape of Qualitative Research: Theories and Issues*. 2nd edn.. London: SAGE. pp. 1–45.

Dickey, M.D. (2003) '3D virtual worlds: an emerging technology for traditional and distance learning', paper presented at the Convergence of Learning and Technology Conference, Columbus, OH, March. Retrieved 19 August 2008, from www.oln.org/conferences/OLN2003/papers/Dickey3DVirtualWorlds.pdf

Dovey, J. and Kennedy, H.W. (2006) *Game Cultures: Computer Games as New Media*. Maidenhead: Open University Press.

Gee, J.P. (2004) *What Videogames Have to Teach Us about Learning and Literacy*. New York: Palgrave Macmillan.

Ingram, A.L., Hathorn, L.G. and Evans, A. (2000) 'Beyond chat on the internet', *Computers and Education*, 35(1): 21–35.

Holloway, S. and Valentine, G. (2002) Cyberkids: Children in the Information Age. London: RoutledgeFalmer.

Lankshear,C. and Knobel, M. (2007) *New Literacies: Changing Knowledge and Classroom Learning*. Buckingham: Open University Press.

Lim, C.P., Nonis, D. and Hedberg, J. (2006) 'Gaming in a 3D multiuser environment: engaging students in science lessons', *British Journal of Educational Technology*, 37(2): 211–31.

Merchant, G. (2007a) 'Digital writing in the early years', in J. Coiro, M. Knobel, C. Lankshear and D. Leu (eds), *New Literacies Research Handbook*. Mawah, NJ: Lawrence Erlbaum. pp. 755–78.

Merchant, G. (2007b) 'Writing the future', *Literacy*, 41(3): 1–19.

Pratt, M.L. (1991) 'Arts of the contact zone', *Profession*, 91(4): 33–40.

Primary Framework (2007) *The Primary Framework: Learning Objectives for Literacy and Mathematics*. Retrieved 2 January 2008, from www.standards. dfes.gov.uk/primaryframeworks/literacy/learningobjectives/

Rosaldo, R. (1989) *Culture and Truth: The Remaking of Social Analysis*. Boston, MA: Beacon.

Schroeder, R. (2002) 'Social interaction in virtual environments: key issues, common themes, and a framework for research', in R. Schroeder (ed.), *The Social Life of Avatars: Presence and Interaction in Shared Virtual Environments*. London: Springer. pp. 1–19.

Squires, K. (2002) 'Cultural framing of computer/video games', *Game Studies*, 2(1). Retrieved 19 August 2008, from http://gamestudies.org/0102/squire/

Steinkuehler, C. (2007) 'Massively multiplayer online gaming as a constellation of literacy practices', *E-learning*, 4(3): 297–318.

# Download

## Key points

1. Virtual world gameplay involves a wide range of literacy practices, such as onscreen navigation and interactive chat, and encourages online collaboration and learning.
2. The immersive quality of virtual world gameplay can be highly motivating for students, who see these learning environments as more engaging than traditional routines of literacy instruction.
3. Virtual worlds open possibilities for new kinds of relationships between learners, and between learners and their teachers.

## In your classroom

1. Students can visit demonstration virtual worlds such as those at the Active Worlds Education Universe (www.activeworlds.com/edu/awedu.asp).
2. Students can visit popular virtual worlds and critically evaluate their attractiveness and functionality. Some examples are:
   (a) Club Penguin (www.clubpenguin.com)
   (b) Build-a-bear (www.buildabearville.com)
   (c) My Tiny Planets (www.mytinyplanets.com)
3. You can get involved in the educational application of virtual worlds either through Active Worlds (see above) or through Virtually Learning (www.virtuallylearning.co.uk).

## Further reading

Davies, J. and Merchant, G. (in press) *Web 2.0 for Schools: Social Participation and Learning*. New York: Peter Lang.

Schott, G. and Kambouri, M. (2006) 'Social play and learning', in D. Carr, D. Buckingham, A. Burn and G. Schott (eds), *Computer Games: Text, Narrative and Play*. Cambridge: Polity Press. pp. 119–32.

Steinkuehler, C. (2008) 'Cognition and literacy in massively multiplayer online games', in J. Coiro, M. Knobel, C. Lankshear and D. Leu (eds), *Handbook of Research on New Literacies*. Mawah, NJ: Lawrence Erlbaum Associates. pp. 611–34.

# Part C
## Changing literacies, changing pedagogies

The research in this section focuses specifically on teacher education. The preparation of the next generation of classroom teachers and leaders *must* include direct engagement with digital technologies, digital texts and the literacies associated with them. Importantly, these engagements should take place according to the pedagogic model of a learning community that works collaboratively to generate new knowledge. These three chapters report on research in tertiary undergraduate programmes where student-teachers are in training to enter the profession. The chapters set out the parameters of an important, and pending, debate about preparing teachers for the pedagogical work required to productively engage students with changing literacies.

# 7

# Personal Digital Literacies Versus Classroom Literacies: Investigating Pre-service Teachers' Digital Lives in and Beyond the Classroom

## *Cathy Burnett*

Over recent years, there has been much policy rhetoric associated with educational transformation. Digital technology (referred to as 'technology' here) has been seen as key to transforming education through enabling new relationships between teachers and learners and allowing learners to take more control of their own learning process (BECTa, 2006; 2007). While the implications of such transformation for practice are not well defined (see Burnett et al., 2005), it would seem that the interactions that happen through and around digital texts may be significant in achieving this kind of transformation.

Various commentators (Green and Bigum, 2003; Prensky, 2001; Rheingold, 2002) have suggested that immersion in digital environments may lead to new ways of thinking about and using texts, and that it is those who have grown up with digital technology who may be most likely to understand the potential of digital affordances. From this perspective, it may be that the new generation of teachers is well placed to develop innovative uses of new technology in the classroom. Young and pre-service teachers may have gained valuable understandings about digital texts through their previous and continuing use of digital environments. However, there has been little research directly related to pre-service teachers' own digital literacy or the relationships between this and their developing professional role. Research into pre-service teachers' technology use has tended to focus on their skills in using what may be described as work-related applications, such as word-processing and data-handling. Mayo et al. (2005), for example, evaluated programmes designed to embed support for students' use of technology more effectively within initial teacher education (ITE). Banister and Vannatta (2005) focused on audits of pre-service teachers' skill, whereas Topper (2004) surveyed students' confidence in using technology. While useful in considering how technology is mediated within ITE, such studies have not investigated the nature or extent of pre-service teachers' more informal playful interactions with digital texts such as texting, computer gaming, blogging or social networking.

Robinson and Mackey (2006) have made links between pre-service teachers' personal use of technology and classroom application. Their conclusions reflect those from other studies, which have highlighted the dangers of making assumptions about young people's ease and expertise in digital environments (Facer et al, 2001; Holloway and Valentine, 2002). Robinson and Mackey caution against assuming that pre-service teachers are 'insiders' to the full range of digital technology; the pre-service teachers they surveyed rarely used certain technologies, such as computer games. Users had varying degrees of access and levels of confidence when using different applications, or with different aspects of digital literacy. The significance of digital experience may not simply be within the skills pre-service teachers bring to ITE but the values, attitudes and assumptions associated with that use, and the ways these intersect with those apparent within classrooms.

In exploring the potential for pre-service teachers to draw from prior experience of digital technology, it would seem important to know more about their experience of digital texts in different domains of their lives. Rather than focusing on their skills in using technology, it is helpful to conceptualize their encounters with digital technologies, including those that surround digital texts, as 'digital practices'. Drawing from ethnographic studies, which have explored literacy practices within different contexts (see Barton and Hamilton, 1998; Scribner and Cole, 1981), a focus on textual practices involves examining what people *do* with texts. In addition to logging the kinds of texts produced or consumed, this means investigating the values, priorities, purposes and feelings associated with these texts, and the places, spaces, relationships, interactions and processes which characterize their use. In effect, looking at digital experience as practice may provide insights into the discourses that frame this experience in different domains. Such insights may be helpful in both highlighting possible ways in which they may support transformative uses of technology and understanding the barriers that may inhibit such developments.

This chapter reports on findings from a study, which aimed to explore pre-service teachers' digital lives within and beyond initial teacher education. By investigating their digital practices, the study investigated the way that pre-service teachers *experience* their use of digital texts and the value they and others place on their use. It focused both on pre-service teachers' experience beyond ITE and the experiences and attitudes encountered as they tried to integrate technology in the classroom.

# Research design

Seven female pre-service teachers were interviewed for this study. All participants were pre-service teachers in the second year of a three-year undergraduate course of primary initial teacher education at a university in northern England. A series of three individual, semi-structured interviews were used to investigate the values and significance they attributed to the use of digital texts in various domains, including their university and school-based experience. Prior to the first interview, they completed mindmaps (Buzan and Buzan, 1993) representing their experience of using digital texts, commenting on how they used them and how these uses were significant to them. During the first set of interviews, they were asked to talk through the ideas represented on their maps. The second interviews explored their experiences during school placement. They focused on teachers they had encountered and described how they used digital texts in their professional role. Following analysis of these interviews a third round was conducted, during which students were invited to reflect more fully on how digital texts had been used in their university-based training and to expand on their experience of using digital texts in their own lives. Systematic inductive analysis was used throughout the process to both characterize individual pre-service teachers' experiences of digital literacy and identify themes generated by the data. This involved repeated readings of the interview transcripts to identify and develop emerging themes. Participants were also invited to review and comment upon the interpretation of their experience.

Here, the focus is on four of the younger participants: Kathryn, Holly, Joanne and Kate. Pen portraits of these four students are provided here as an attempt to capture insight into their digital practices at the time of the study.

## Kathryn

Kathryn is 20 years old and comes from the North East of England. She sees herself as a confident user of digital technology. Moving away from home to come to university has meant leaving her very close family. When she first arrived she set up a webcam, which she used for webchats with her mother, and used MSN extensively to communicate with her brother. She has a particular interest in fashion, and considered a career in this area; during her holidays she works in a women's clothes shop and advises the owner on recent trends researched using the internet. Recently she set up her own homepage on Facebook, after being encouraged to do so by a friend. She describes herself as an 'observer' rather than a contributor, enjoying lurking on others' pages rather than adding to her own. Nevertheless she is a digital archivist, retaining all her emails and messages on her Facebook 'wall' and revisiting messages she feels are important. She is committed to her own professional development and has achieved highly in her academic work, supporting her independent study using online resources. As part of her course, she also accesses the university's virtual learning environment in order to find resources.

*Continued*

*Continued*

She has visited a number of online discussion boards designed to facilitate peer and tutor support for assignment preparation. She is frequently irritated by the kinds of questions posted by others, which she feels could easily be resolved in other ways.

## Joanne

Joanne is 24 years old and has been employed in a variety of jobs outside education before starting her course, including work at a post office, a restaurant, and a leisure centre. She lives with her partner and works hard to maintain her strong network of friends and family. Recently, for example, she bought a mobile phone for her partner's mother. This enabled her to stay in constant contact and provide emotional support. Joanne moves between various modes of communication as she maintains contact with different friends and family members, using email, txting, or phone calls as she feels best suits each situation. She uses the internet extensively to save time, and enjoys receiving the multimedia text messages sent by her partner (who she feels is far more 'romantic' in text messages than in real life). She is very committed to her future career in teaching, and cites her love of children as her main motivation. She has recently been introduced by fellow students to Facebook, and is fascinated by the new communities that have formed there. She talks frequently about her lack of confidence and suggests that this is why, like Kathryn, she positions herself very much as a passive contributor, although the practices she describes suggest that she is actually highly competent in negotiating new environments. She is similarly reluctant to contribute to university-based online discussion boards, feeling that her contributions may be viewed negatively by other students.

## Holly

Holly is 20 years old and shares a house with her partner. Like Kathryn, she has moved away from home to come to university, and uses digital communication to keep in touch with family and friends. She also associates different practices with different relationships. For example, she has a school friend who is hearing impaired with whom she exchanges lengthy text messages to keep in touch while away at university. Holly is a keen user of social networking sites and, online, feels she manages to maintain the identity she developed while at school. She is interested in music and uses the Internet to keep up to date with bands from the USA. She also books her holidays using the web as this enables her to create holidays suited to her needs and interests. She is amused by the way in which her older relatives, ranging from her enthusiastic grandparents to her reluctant mother, use digital technology.

*Continued*

*Continued*

## Kate

Kate is also 20. Like the others, she uses digital communication flexibly, responding to the preferences of others. She knows, for example, that her father prefers email but hates his mobile phone, so she always emails him while she texts his wife. She uses her own mobile phone extensively, texting people to avoid interrupting their lives. She exchanges frequent texts with her boyfriend, who she feels needs this constant contact. She, however, prefers a phone call as she feels this is more personal. As a key figure in the local youth theatre, she uses email to organize and manage others, feeling that this enables her to fulfil her role while keeping the demands manageable. Like Joanne, she has recently started using Facebook and is intrigued by this new environment. She dislikes MSN but does find herself using it because her partner uses it, and consequently it is activated when she comes to use her personal computer (PC) at home. She is amused by the way that others mistake her for him. Despite the confidence with which she negotiates her digital relationships with family, friends and colleagues, she expressed some uncertainty about the conventions for more formal emails such as those directed to university-based tutors.

## Kathryn, Holly, Joanne and Kate: their digital lives beyond the classroom

None of these students identified themselves as having particular skills in using digital technology. In fact, they sometimes took pains to distance themselves from those they saw as technically proficient. Joanne, for example, described herself as 'not computer literate', while Holly asserted that she was 'not a geek'. 'Computer literacy' seemed to be associated with detailed knowledge of equipment rather than the uses to which that equipment is put. Moreover, as in Robinson and Mackey's (2006) study, the range of their experience could be seen as limited. All used the internet, including social networking sites, instant messaging, email and text messages, although the extent and enthusiasm with which they used each varied. All were suspicious of virtual worlds, none played computer games and, apart from their experimentation with FaceBook, none had engaged in any form of online publishing, for example through blogging, wikis or website creation. Notably, their explorations of new environments seemed to be brokered by friends and families, and aimed to reinforce those relationships rather than develop new ones; they seemed to enjoy using digital environments to find new ways of being within existing relationships. Indeed, they at times expressed suspicion regarding environments with which they were not familiar. For example, all had tried to enter an online virtual world in response to a seminar discussion, but all had backed out once faced with the prospect of entering personal details. Various reasons were given for this reluctance, ranging from a lack of confidence about how to navigate the environment or behave once inside, to a suspicion that this may not be a place that would welcome them or, worse still, that they may be pulled into an environment beyond their control.

These pre-service teachers did not then seem to engage in the kinds of digital practices that might be associated with more transformative modes of learning. They had not, for example, experienced the possibilities for identity play and experimentation that might be possible in a virtual world. They had little experience of developing an online presence, or of the possibilities for knowledge creation and knowledge-sharing that might accompany this, and their online practices seemed to reinforce existing relationships rather than develop new ones. It initially seemed that their digital practices were purely functional; they used digital technology to achieve existing purposes, such as communication or information retrieval, more efficiently. This apparent reluctance to experiment seemed a long way from the kind of confidence that might be associated with being a 'digital native' (Prensky, 2001), and this could suggest that their experience had little relevance to supporting a transformative agenda in the classroom.

However, as their descriptions of their practices elaborated how they used what they did and why it was significant to them, it became evident that all four pre-service teachers had extensive experience using digital texts flexibly and with agency in their everyday lives. There were aspects of their practices that would indeed seem to have provided them with understandings that could be relevant to using digital technology to transform classroom practice. As they described their digital lives, they outlined how they adopted different roles and orientated themselves towards texts in different ways. Their participation in digital environments seemed to enable them to shift easily between multiple identities; as old friend, new friend, student, colleague, peer, daughter or mother.

These students' digital practices did not simply surround their own needs or interests. They all, for example, talked about ways that key events in their lives (such as moving to university or the death of a relative) prompted them to introduce new technologies to others in their family, particularly those who were older than them. It was evident that their digital practices were not fixed, and that their relationships often provided the contexts through which they were introduced to new digital environments. During the course of this study, both Kate and Joanne were introduced to the social networking site, Facebook. They described how friends had introduced them to the site, and the excitement they had experienced when they realized that it was already peopled by those they knew. At the time of the study, they were beginning to experiment with ways of being and operating within the new environment. There was a real playfulness both in what they described and the way they discussed this in interview. These were students who were keen to explore and experiment, and moved between operating as mentors to some and apprentices to others.

It is possible that these pre-service teachers' experiences beyond the classroom could be of real value to them in their professional lives. While none identified themselves as having particularly strong competence using technology, they suggested a degree of technical skill, and an ease with creating multimodal texts and using language in diverse ways within digital environments. Such strengths could be extremely valuable to them in delivering the current primary curriculum with its new emphasis on supporting children in reading and writing screen-based texts (Primary National Strategy, 2006), and the requirement that teachers should draw from digital resources in their teaching (Training and Development Agency for Schools, 2007). However, their accounts suggested that their experiences had equipped them to do more than this. They had all adopted different identities within digital environments, and were aware of the ways in which digital texts can mediate different kinds of relationships. Their own experience of moving flexibly between roles as teachers and learners of digital practices seemed to exemplify participation in a learning community in which responsibility was shared and experience pooled. Such experience could equip them to consider ways in which teacher–learner relationships could be reconfigured, and to find practical ways of using technology transformatively in the classroom.

This is, of course, speculative. Such transference would depend both on the students' own capacity to identify opportunities for innovation and the way that such innovation was encouraged in school. It could be seen to depend, in effect, on the extent to which these experiences were seen to be relevant to the school environment, or aligned to the discourses encountered in the classroom. Against this background, it is interesting to see how teachers responded to these students' attempts to use digital technology in the classroom.

## Digital life in the school environment

These students' accounts of the flexible and agential ways in which they engaged with digital technology beyond their ITE course contrasted with how they described their uses of digital technology within the school environment. The students' presentation of their classroom experience suggested that schools, and individual teachers within them, were at different stages in their integration of technology within the curriculum. These different stages were evident in:

- the amount and kinds of technologies available;
- the frequency with which they were used;
- the access that was possible to digital technologies; and
- the way in which ICT had been framed within the curriculum.

It is notable that the digital technologies that these students engaged with at school were significantly different to those that they engaged with in their wider lives. The students described no incidents where children worked in classrooms from laptops or used mobile technologies. Apart from one mention of a digital camera, no other digital technology was mentioned by any of the interviewees. All students referred to classrooms where opportunities to use digital technology were scarce, and computers were marginalized and even neglected. Students spoke of weekly timetabled slots in computer suites, and classroom PCs covered in layers of dust and debris. All described at least one teacher who had readily confessed their lack of expertise in using technology, and in these cases the task of operating equipment was delegated to teaching assistants or children, or ICT was addressed through decontextualized exercises taken from a published scheme.

Other teachers were described as confident and even inspirational users of technology in the classroom. However, nearly all of the 'inspirational' practices cited focused on the use of technology to support established classroom practices. Most examples of technology use related to electronic whiteboards, which appeared to be used mainly for teacher-led whole-class teaching. While digital texts were used to stimulate or motivate children, the main focus of activities was apparently still very much teacher-led. The students did describe instances where the internet had been accessed in class. However, in virtually all cases, this was used to access online educational games or information selected by the teacher. Web pages were displayed on electronic whiteboards with the teacher acting as gatekeeper, framing and directing children's encounters.

Against this background, Kate, Holly, Kathryn and Joanne drew from their knowledge of technology to support their classroom practice. Committed to their own professional development, they all sought to use digital technologies during their placements. In doing so, they used the technologies and models that were readily available to them, and it is not the purpose of this chapter to comment on the value of what they did. However, the way that these attempts were regarded is suggestive of the extent to which their personal digital expertise was valued, and how they were encouraged to draw from this experience. Their reactions to such responses help us to explore the way they brokered the feedback they received. Both negative and positive responses provide insights here.

Kathryn, for example, described the reaction of one of her teachers to her arrangements for using an interactive whiteboard in another classroom to show the children a website.

> Kathryn: ... when I had to take them down, when I told the teacher he was quite against that.
> Cathy: Really? What happened?
> Kathryn: He was sort of saying, 'Why do you need to do that? Why do you need to move them? Can you not just do it on the overhead projector?' I could have done but I just wanted to do ... I wanted to have a go at using the interactive whiteboard because I felt like I've had no practice on it and it's

one of your targets, it's one of the standards you've got to meet … but just the sort of reaction from him was almost enough to think, 'should I be bothering'.

In this case, the teacher's reaction does little to encourage Kathryn to utilize technology at all, let alone prompt her to explore more transformative ways of using technology. Interestingly, she does not see the teacher's response as valid, but as blocking her progress towards the professional standards she must meet. By commenting, 'it's one of your targets', Kathryn frames her frustration in terms of the standards that pre-service teachers are required to meet during initial teacher education (Teacher Development Agency for Schools, 2007; Teacher Training Agency, 2003). She almost seems to refer to these for endorsement that her intentions were right. While she was frustrated by her experience, she is able to dismiss the teacher's reaction as inappropriate and remains enthusiastic about using technology. She may have lost control over her own development during this practice, but remains in control of her ideas about the kind of teacher she wants, or feels she is required, to be. Her ability to find external endorsement for her intended approach sustains her; the standards require her to use technology in her teaching so she remains convinced this is appropriate. However, it is interesting that her convictions relate to a lesson in which she was to use the electronic whiteboard to enable children to access a website. Her intentions are to motivate children and enliven her lesson, very much in line with the discourses of primary teaching, which perhaps emphasize teacher control achieved alongside, or through, the engagement of pupils.

For other students, the negative reactions they encounter may be framed in ways that they find harder to disregard. Kate, for example, commented on her initial visits to her forthcoming placement school. She anticipated that she would have few opportunities for integrating technology within practice. She felt that this was not necessarily caused by a lack of teacher expertise, but because it would counteract the teachers' pedagogical aims:

> Kate: They're trying to work in a sort of hands-on, creative way, and I think, in their minds, IT [information technology] doesn't do that because they're more interested in developing motor skills and things like that. And also there's a big thing about the children being able to socially interact well and communicate with each other, which if they were stuck with computers all the time, they might be inhibited a bit … so … yeah, I don't think they use ICT really much in the classroom.

Her comments here are interesting and suggest a lack of certainty about whether or not these teachers' views are justified. As she explains their position – a rejection of IT as this may inhibit creativity – she seems to distance herself from their views: 'I think, *in their minds*, IT doesn't do that because they're more interested in developing motor skills and things like that' [my italics]. However, as she continues to describe their principles, there seems to be a sense that she acknowledges their concerns: 'and also there's a big thing about the children being able to socially interact well and communicate with each other, *which if*

*they were stuck with computers all the time, they might be inhibited a bit'* [my italics].
Of course this view of the social interaction associated with computers can be
challenged, and on reflection, Kate, a critically reflective student, may well have
begun to question these teachers' approach (and indeed her own assumption that
technology use must involve children being 'stuck at computers all the time').
However, there is a sense that she is following the reasoning presented to her, and
perhaps that, in order to survive within this new placement environment at least,
she will have to adapt to it. Here, she finds that ideas developed during her course
are incompatible with the practices of her teacher/mentor.

While Kate and Kathryn's attempts to integrate technology within their teaching were rejected by their teachers, the students did describe incidents where
they had been given credit for the way in which they used technology within
the classroom. Holly, for example, described how she had shown her class
teacher how to email plans between home and school.

> Holly: I showed her how to email it to herself. She didn't have to carry a disk
> about but send it as an attachment on an email and pick it up at school and
> just download it all.
> Cathy: And what did she think of that?
> Holly: She thought it was brilliant because she'd seen us doing it and she was
> like, 'oh, how've you done that?' We were, 'we've just emailed it because we
> don't want to be messing about with disks' … because a CD, once you've
> used it, that's it, 'well, I'll throw it away now'.
> Cathy: You said you thought she wasn't very keen. What was it that she did
> or said that suggested that?
> Holly: She told us. She said, 'I don't know anything about computers – show
> me everything.' She said, 'I don't know anything. We've had a half hour
> training session on how to use the whiteboard and that's it.'
> Cathy: At what point did she say that to you?
> Holly: Pretty early on. She was a great teacher. She was really open about
> everything: 'I don't know how to do this? I don't know how to do that. Show
> me.'
> Cathy: And how did that feel to you?
> Holly: Pretty good actually. Like, well, she's been teaching for like 20 odd
> years and she knows all this stuff and then we come in and we've just been
> a few months on this course but we know something that she doesn't. Kind
> of like, 'we know something'. At first, like all the teaching we were doing, we
> felt really nervous but then because, OK, teachers aren't these superhuman
> creatures who know everything. They do make mistakes and don't know
> everything. It felt really good.

Holly felt encouraged to share her expertise and seemed to welcome this. The
fact that she was awarded the status of expert seemed to reinforce her own
sense of credibility; her expertise was seen as relevant and significant to her in
her professional development. Moreover, she felt that the act of sharing
empowered her to feel that she had something to give. This seemed to enhance
her sense of her own credibility and enable her to feel she could make a real
contribution within the school within which she was placed. Unlike the

examples cited above, in this situation Holly is made to feel that she can bring new ideas to the classroom.

Significantly, however, the skills she was applauded for here were technical skills and, moreover, they were used to support her professional role rather than her interactions with children. She was not praised for using her awareness of networked technology to create new learning contexts for children, but to support her own efficiency within her professional role. This reflects examples cited by other students who described teachers' use of texting and email to share resources and planning. Here, digital technology supports a network of teachers who are perhaps finding new ways to collaborate mediated by digital technology. These teachers are using the network to ensure they are prepared and consistent, but ultimately this seems aimed at achieving a more standardized approach to planning and teaching. This new way of working (or enacting professionalism) perhaps reinforces the existing structures which frame teaching and learning in the classroom.

The emphasis on standardized and directed teaching was also evident within the students' descriptions of lessons during which their technology use had been applauded. Joanne, for example, described a PowerPoint she produced to support children's learning of their multiplication tables:

> Joanne: And when it was the World Cup, I was doing a numeracy lesson, I'd made this football picture on one of the PowerPoint slides. I managed to get proper football shirts with the numbers they were times-ing by and if they got it right, I managed to put some sound on and it said 'goal' and all that. I remember Clare [the class teacher] really enjoyed that. She said that it was great because the kids enjoyed it and spoke to me about it afterwards and wanted to do it. Even if they'd done it, they wanted to play it. I think it is because it was up there and it was all colourful.

Joanne's use of PowerPoint seemed to represent a genuine commitment to finding imaginative and relevant ways to support children in reaching the specified objective. Her internet research, and skills in creating multimodal texts, enabled her to create a resource which involved the children in consolidating skills relevant to the current mathematics curriculum. Through using this PowerPoint, she effectively remains 'in control' of the children, who she sees as motivated by the multimodal presentation. The children were entertained by the PowerPoint, but Joanne was in control of the text. The PowerPoint was created prior to the lesson so, while slides could be deleted or skipped, the path to learning was determined without the children. She has designed it and orchestrates the children's interactions with it. Importantly, in this example, Joanne's skills in manipulating digital texts again seemed to have afforded her credibility. Her description suggests that she felt she gained approval from her class teacher, who saw her use of technology as successful and appropriate. However, the success of the text produced is judged in terms of the children's motivation rather than their learning. The value, to the class teacher, of her competence in using digital texts appeared to be in the way she was able to create a text that engaged the children within teacher-directed whole-class teaching.

These students then experienced varying levels of encouragement when attempting to integrate technology in their classroom practice. When they were encouraged, this was often because they were succeeding within the current curriculum, and their uses of technology fitted within existing classroom discourses; their classroom practice upheld, and rarely challenged, traditional relationships between teachers and learners. Positive feedback was given for lessons in which they had managed to engage children through technological wizardry, thus maintaining 'control' over the class. In such contexts, they seem to have used their experience of creating and accessing digital texts in preparing resources to support the existing curriculum.

It is hardly surprising that these students had not drawn from digital practices developed beyond initial teacher education to attempt to re-frame the curriculum. Student-teachers are likely to learn about what might be possible from the models they encounter, and there was no evidence here that any had encountered practices that could be described as transformative. Indeed, studies of teacher professional development suggest that students achieve the greatest recognition, and perhaps feel most successful, when they effectively align themselves to existing practices within a school (see Britzman, 2003; Craig, 2000). When asked specifically why they thought they had not seen or planned for a broader range of technologies, such as children's own use of digital communication, the participants variously suggested different kinds of tensions within existing classroom practice. Some described the possible safety risks involved in giving children increased access to networked technology, while others expressed concerns that children would stray off task if allowed to engage in unstructured web-based activities. For other students, the prescriptive curriculum and emphasis on achieving certain standards in national tests militated against an environment where ownership of the technology rested with the children. This took precedence and prevented the kind of flexibility and autonomy associated with experimentation within digital environments.

## Transformation through digital practices: barriers and opportunities

There is no attempt here to suggest that the experiences of these four pre-service teachers were typical. Their experiences in and out of school were patterned by their particular values, relationships, preferences and interests, and by the opportunities they had been given within placement schools. Similar investigations related to students in other courses, or with different kinds of prior, informal or school experience may have yielded very different insights. Notably, in this study, all the interviewees were female, and it is possible that their focus on digital texts as mediators of relationships, and their enthusiasm for particular kinds of social networking, were gendered responses.

Nevertheless, their stories of digital practices within and beyond the classroom do raise questions about the ways that prior and informal digital experience filter into courses of initial teacher education.

Focusing on practices, rather than auditing skills and competences, has highlighted some of the tensions that exist for pre-service teachers. It has emphasized the way that these pre-service teachers positioned themselves differently through their uses of digital technology in different contexts. This suggests that the introduction of equipment or new, networked opportunities in classrooms will offer little transformative potential unless this is accompanied by a challenge to dominant discourses. It is not the technology itself that creates the opportunities for transformation, but the way it is inflected by and related to other practices that happen within that environment.

In their own lives, digital practices were notable for their flexibility and temporality. The pre-service teachers moved between positions of expertise and inexperience as they negotiated their way through different environments, sometimes as learners and sometimes as teachers. They positioned themselves within a web of relationships, and shifting identities and associated concerns, values, priorities and enthusiasms patterned their practices. In the classroom, however, they were engaged in a very particular task, that of negotiating a professional identity. It is not surprising, therefore, that the way in which they draw from their digital experience was refracted through the discourses they encountered. They used the kinds of skills that they developed beyond the classroom, but used them in ways that fitted with dominant modes of teacher-directed and objective-driven learning.

In this study, a focus on digital practices has helped highlight the variety of factors that influence the way pre-service teachers view the role of new technologies within different domains. These students engaged in wide-ranging practices beyond school, which demonstrated their creativity and confidence in using digital technology within different contexts. Other students will engage in their own particular digital practices, which will be inflected by the relationships, interests, places and pressures that are significant to them. It is likely, however, that the attitudes, values and understandings developed through such practices may well be relevant to their professional lives. Reflecting on such practices may provide the critical distance from current classroom practice needed to begin to consider ways of achieving a more transformative education.

These findings clearly have implications for teacher educators who must find ways of encouraging pre-service teachers to evaluate current practices surrounding digital technology in the classroom. However, they also have implications for pre-service teachers themselves. They highlight the need for pre-service teachers to reflect critically on the discourses that underpin classroom activity. As this study suggests, contrasting digital practices within and beyond the classroom may provide a useful starting point for this. Such reflection may enable pre-service teachers to better understand the factors which structure classroom learning, and to consider ways through which they can work within those structures to challenge them.

# References

Banister, S. and Vannatta, R. (2005) 'Beginning with a baseline: insuring productive technology integration in teacher education', *Journal of Technology and Teacher Education*, 14(1): 209–35.

Barton, D. and Hamilton, M. (1998) *Local Literacies*. London: Routledge.

British Educational Communications and Technology Agency (BECTa) (2006) *Emerging Technologies for Learning: Volume 1*. Retrieved 11 April 2007, from http://partners.becta.org.uk/index.php?section=rh&catcode=_re_rp_ap_03&rid=11380

British Educational Communications and Technology Agency (BECTa) (2007) *Emerging Technologies for Learning: Volume 2*. Retrieved 11 April 2007, from http://partners.becta.org.uk/index.php?section=rh&catcode=_re_rp_ap_03&rid=11380

Britzman, D.P. (2003) *Practice Makes Practice: A Critical Study of Learning to Teach*. New York: State University of New York Press.

Burnett, C., Dickinson, P., Merchant, G. and Myers, J. (2005) 'Digital connections: transforming literacy in the primary school', *Cambridge Review of Education*, 36(1): 11–29.

Buzan, T. and Buzan, B. (1993) *The Mind Map Book*. London: BBC Books.

Craig, C. (2000) 'Stories of schools/teacher stories: a 2-part invention on the walls theme', *Curriculum Inquiry*, 30(1): 12–41.

Facer, K., Furlong, J., Furlong, R. and Sutherland, S. (2001) 'Constructing the child computer user: from public policy to private practices', *British Journal of Sociology of Education*, 22(1): 91–108.

Green, B. and Bigum, C. (2003) 'Aliens in the classroom', *Australian Journal of Education*, 37(2): 119–41.

Holloway, S. and Valentine, G. (2002) *Cyberkids: Youth Identities and Communities in an On-line World*. London: RoutledgeFalmer.

Mayo, N.B., Kajs, L.T. and Tanguma, J. (2005) 'Longitudinal study of technology training to prepare future teachers', *Education Research Quarterly*, 29(1): 3–16.

Prensky, M. (2001) *Digital Natives, Digital Immigrants* [electronic version]. Retrieved 15 December 2005, from www.marcprensky.com/writing/Prensky

Primary National Strategy (2006) *Primary Framework for Literacy*. Retrieved 28 April 2008, from www.standards.dfes.gov.uk/primaryframework/literacy/

Rheingold, H. (2002) *Smart Mob: The Next Social Revolution Transforming Cultures and Communities in the Age of Instant Access*. New York: Basic Books.

Robinson, M. and Mackey, M. (2006) 'Assets in the classroom: comfort and competence with media among teachers present and future', in J. Marsh and E. Millard (eds), *Popular Literacies, Childhood and Schooling*. London: Routledge. pp. 200–20.

Scribner, S. and Cole, M. (1981) *The Psychology of Literacy*. Cambridge, MA: Harvard University Press.

Teacher Training Agency (2003) *Qualifying to Teach: Professional Standards for Qualified Teacher Status and Requirements of Initial Teacher Training*. London: TTA.

Topper, A. (2004) 'How are we doing? Using self-assessment to measure changing teacher technology literacy within a graduate educational technology program', *Journal of Technology and Teacher Education*, 12(3): 303–18.

Training and Development Agency for Schools (2007) *QTS Standards*. Retrieved 28 April 2008, from www.tda.gov.uk/partners.aspx

# Download

## Key points

1. Digital practices are framed by the discourses that prevail in different domains. Consequently, in schools, digital technology is often assimilated into existing classroom relationships and student-teachers are likely to be encouraged when they support this assimilation.
2. Examining technology use as 'practice' highlights the barriers and opportunities to using technology in ways that could challenge existing relationships between teachers and learners.
3. Digital practices beyond formal educational contexts are frequently characterized by flexibility, variety, agency, and embedded in real-life purposes and events. In contrast, technology may be used in the classroom in decontextualized ways that reinforce transmission models of learning.

## In your classroom

1. Reflect upon the range and scope of your own digital practices. Consider the kinds of language, activities and attitudes that you associate with different technologies and digital texts. Also, consider how you learned to use different technologies and the conditions which facilitated this learning. Consider how this experience might be valuable to you in your professional role.
2. Observe technology use in classrooms you know and visit. Consider: relationships between teachers, learners, and technology; availability, location, and range of equipment; and curriculum priorities and contexts for learning. Which values and priorities seem to underpin classroom technology use? How far does technology enable learners to take control of their own learning?
3. Research the digital practices of a group of children in your classroom, perhaps using mindmapping as a starting point. What does this tell you about the skills, attitudes, values, and understandings they bring to classroom technology use? How could you plan to acknowledge, draw from, and extend these?

## Further reading

Barton, D. and Hamilton, M. (1998) *Local Literacies*. London: Routledge.

Burnett, C., Dickinson, P., Merchant, G. and Myers, J. (2005) 'Digital connections: transforming literacy in the primary school', *Cambridge Review of Education*, 36(1): 11–29.

Graham, L. (2008) 'Teachers are digikids too: the digital histories and digital lives of young teachers in English primary schools', *Literacy*, 42(1): 10–18.

# Digital Portraits: Teacher Education and Multiliteracies Pedagogy

*Rosie Kerin*

## Introduction: digital literacies and student-teachers

Over the past twenty years, educators and policy-makers across developed and developing nations have witnessed and unevenly grappled with the rapid development of digital technologies, including the expansion of the internet and Web 2.0 technologies, wireless connectivity, and the development of computer applications and hardware that have simplified the construction of multimodal texts and interaction. Research exploring the impact of such technologies in relation to literacy education has been growing exponentially, and there are now substantial accounts of how some systems and individual educators are responding to the demands and challenges within schools and classrooms (see for example, Alvermann et al., 2006; Durrant and Beavis, 2001; Evans, 2005; Kist, 2005; Marsh and Millard, 2006). In addition to systematic research conducted with educators and learners, further challenges have been presented for educators, including calls to develop 'insider' mindsets (Lankshear and Knobel, 2003), to enrich educational experiences of young people by learning from the design and appeal of online video games (Gee, 2003) or to rethink education in light of 'a commodity-saturated world where the boundaries between media and text, public and private, work and leisure are increasingly blurred' (Carrington, 2006, p. 172).

The advent of digital technologies has also precipitated a move from consumer to producer dispositions with recognition of the 'participatory potential of new technologies' (Buckingham, 2003, p. 14), constituting a challenge in educational contexts which have traditionally constructed students as readers and synthesisers rather than creators or designers of knowledge or ideas. Kress (2000) argues that the notion of design has led to 'a quite new, radically different theory of meaning, of semiosis, in which the individual is always shaping ... and never simply "using", as in "language users"' (p. 143). Design draws on the multimodalities afforded by digital technology, such as the use of image and hyperlink in web pages, or the manipulation of image, sound and text in moving images (Jewitt and Kress, 2003; Kress, 2003). While universities have long privileged communication in the form of academic writing, the concepts of multimodality and design offer challenges to teacher educators, charged with the preparation of future generations of literacy teachers who will work with young people immersed and productive within a multimodal digital culture where the image and screen replace print and page as the dominant form of communication (Kress, 2003).

Given this broader context, this chapter contributes to the smaller but significant body of research that takes a step back from school settings, and examines the digital experiences and dispositions of student-teachers within university settings. In their study of student-teacher 'comfort and competence with media in the classroom', Robinson and Mackey (2006) concluded that 'somewhat worryingly, in the UK at least, we found that many pre-service teachers have a very functional view of the place of new media and the way that such media might play a part in education' (p. 213). Another UK study carried out by Loveless et al. (2006), explored the responses of student-teachers to the pedagogical demands of exploring creativity through the process of working with children on the construction of digital films. Despite the fact that these student-teachers were all ICT specialists, they experienced technical frustrations and challenges relating to completing tasks on time, themes that will emerge within this chapter, and 'expressed their initial anxieties in being "given permission" to work in open-ended activities which seemed to contradict their previous experience of more prescribed planning for specific outcomes' (Loveless et al., 2006, p. 12). Similarly, a Norwegian study (Krumsvik, 2006) explored the place of digital technologies in teacher education, and did so in the belief that despite the rhetoric of a digital revolution in well resourced schools, very little had actually changed:

> In many ways the school's context has changed radically over the last decade, but at the same time we can see that the school fumbles in its response to this development, and remains static and protected against technology, even if the students 'bathe' in technology in their leisure time. (p. 244)

Krumsvik argues that teacher education must embrace new 'epistemological contours' and accept that what knowledge is, and how it is accessed and constructed, is fundamentally altered within digital environments (2006, p. 253), and that the development of student-teacher digital literacies is a necessary step in the preparation of teachers who have the capacity 'to actually experience where the technology gives added value and where it is redundant' (2006, p. 253).

In her exploration of the digital life histories of teachers, Graham (2008) developed categories of teachers according to their experiences and learning with digital technologies, and while there were overlaps and finer distinctions, two key categories she described are the 'serious solitary' learner who engaged with technologies for work purposes, and the 'playful social' learner of digital technologies whose social interactions and pleasure were integral to their mastery of, and confidence with, digital literacies. Graham argues that education can be enriched by the contributions of new 'playful social' teachers because these are the 'first generation of young teachers to have had the possibility of playful social learning in their social lives' (2008, p. 17). Doherty (2007) reaches a similar conclusion in her study of 'masterclass pedagogy' in teacher education in her Australian context, suggesting that younger student-teachers are more adept and comfortable with new technologies. Acknowledging the importance of 'doing as we say', she embarked on a process of explicitly teaching and modelling as her class engaged in the construction and deconstruction of digital texts during their elective unit in the application of new technologies in education. In her conclusion, Doherty argued that 'the ground may have shifted from early efforts to address multimedia applications for the pre-service teacher. Many of our younger recruits to the profession have grown up in a digital ecology, so we can move on from crisis scenarios to more conscious pedagogic enrichment' (2007, p. 325). While many younger 'recruits' to the teaching profession have indeed grown up in a digital ecology, a significant challenge for teacher educators, and educators more broadly, is that this is not exclusively the case, and technical proficiency is only one aspect of the inclusion of digital texts within the context of teacher education.

The student-teacher cohort at the heart of this chapter completed an English Language and Literacy course of ten weeks duration in 2006. A key assessment task was the completion of a 'digital portrait' of a learner. This digital portrait, exploring the in- and out-of-school literacies of a young learner, was constructed using PowerPoint and blended photographs, voice-over, and references to readings and lectures within the course. Within this group of student-teachers there was a broad diversity of age, as well as experience of, access to and disposition in relation to digital technologies. Not all students were comfortable or adept with the technologies required, and many of the comments drawn upon in this chapter reveal levels of frustration or alienation that demand a closer examination of their digital literacies and the context within which they were enacted. In fact, some student evaluations of the course suggest that individuals faced their own 'crisis scenarios' as they attempted to master the software and meet the challenges of the assignment. Within this cohort, several of those students who achieved the highest grades had had no previous experience with the ubiquitous PowerPoint and had felt anxious about their performance on the task. At the same time, for those students who did not meet all of the assessment criteria, it was most often due to an absence of engagement with the key concepts of literacy teaching and learning that were integral to the task, rather than as a direct result of problems mastering the technology.

In this chapter, notions of age and even technical expertise are challenged as key determinants of success and satisfaction with this digital assignment. Rather, a focus on multiliteracies pedagogy (Cope and Kalantzis, 2000; New London Group, 1996), explored below, enables a more expansive and examination of the process that moves beyond technical proficiency to take account of student-teachers' critical engagement with the digital literacies demanded of them in the creation of their digital portraits.

## Multiliteracies pedagogy

The multiliteracies pedagogy (Cope and Kalantzis, 2000; New London Group, 1996) was initially developed in response to a concern about 'what constitutes appropriate literacy teaching in the context of the ever more critical factors of local diversity and global connectedness' (Cope and Kalantzis, 2000, p. 3). The 'multi' prefix was designed to signify two key dimensions of the changing contexts for literacy education: the *multiple* ways of being in the world according to (sub)culture, language, place, and so on; and *multiple* modes of representation available, especially by virtue of new and emerging digital technologies. Globalization, and the advance and spread of digital connectivity via the internet and wireless devices, continues to present new challenges for educators, including teacher educators as we have seen above.

In this chapter, the multiliteracies pedagogy will be used as an analytic lens for the examination of student-teacher reflections on the digital portrait required of them in a literacy course, and will frame possible directions and cautions in relation to the integration of digital literacies in the classroom. Essentially, the multiliteracies pedagogy is made up of four components that must be recognizably present, even though they are interdependent and often overlap, while the absence of one of these components signals a pedagogical shortcoming or deficit. These components are *situated practice, overt instruction, critical framing* and *transformed practice*. The design of teaching and learning that enables the interaction of each of these four components, it is argued, is inclusive, comprehensive and productively relevant in the lives of learners within and beyond their formal educational contexts. These four components will feature in the analysis of student reflections on the digital portrait described in the following section.

## The digital portrait

In 2006, a digital portrait – a visual portrait of a child/adolescent learner constructed in PowerPoint with images, voice-over and accompanying script – was introduced as a key assessment task. Its purpose was to engage a cohort of 176 student-teachers in learning about the in- and out-of-school literacies of one child or adolescent they worked with during practicum. Findings were to be presented in a 10-minute narrated PowerPoint that included images of literate practices, samples of texts used or created by learners, recorded samples of reading or speaking, and observations of the learner within the classroom. In addition, students were directed to include a number of features within their digital profile, including an introduction of the child/adolescent and their educational context, overviews of the child's in- and out-of-school literacies, comments on existing and potential connections between in- and out-of-school literacies, and explicit connections to lectures and readings across the course.

As the assignment task was undertaken by students, it became apparent that despite the ubiquitous presence of PowerPoints in universities and schools many of the student-teachers in the 2006 course had never constructed their own PowerPoint. This was particularly true for mature-age student-teachers, and especially so if they had been out of the workforce or formal education for more than a few years. For those students who had previously mastered the construction of PowerPoints, the inclusion of a voice-over and the insertion of print text in the notes section of PowerPoint added new dimensions. To support all students, regardless of their technical expertise, time was set aside within their regular lectures for a number of weeks to provide students with snap shots of a digital portrait in progress. This gradual construction of a narrated PowerPoint addressing the assignment criteria served as a model for students, and when completed it was posted on the course homepage for their ongoing reference. In addition to informal support from tutors, and via email and online tutorials, three additional and optional workshops were scheduled in a computer laboratory for student-teachers to receive one-on-one technical support in the weeks leading up to the due date.

The inclusion of this assignment in a literacy course, demanding that student-teachers design a text using visuals, print and audio, is consistent with Kress's (2000) argument that literacy education in a digital age demands 'a very different pedagogy and a fundamentally different notion of learning. It sees the learner as fully agentive, as becoming fully aware of the potentials, capacities and affordances of the materials to be used in designs' (p. 141). It should be noted that the assignment demands and criteria were modified slightly in 2007 to allow a broader range of software (iMovie, Photo Story, or Movie Maker) and future iterations will attempt to address the shortcomings and challenges identified in student-teacher responses, the reflections of teachers within the course, and the evolving digital landscape in schools and universities. Further, there exists a tension between the attempt to integrate digital literacies and the maintenance of traditional print assessment practices and expectations, such as full referencing and the submission of the text on disc as well in as in print form for assessment by one individual, namely, the teacher.

## Analysis

At the completion of each course at the University of South Australia, students are invited to submit anonymous course evaluations (Course Evaluation

Instruments – CEI), where they provide reflections on their experiences of the course. Of the 176 students enrolled in the course in 2006, 92 submitted evaluations. The survey invited students to respond to 10 standard statements relating to the quality of the course and to do so according to a scale from 'strongly disagree' to 'strongly agree'. Following these scales, students were provided with an opportunity to add text response answers to these two questions:

11.   Overall, what are the strengths of this course?
12.   Are there any ways this course could be improved?

Of the 92 evaluations received in 2006, 85 provided text responses to questions 11 and 12, and these responses are the key data for this chapter because of the high frequency of statements that related directly to the digital portrait. Table 8.1 provides a simple overview and context for the statements from students extracted from the 2006 data and used in the discussion to follow. In addition, the 2007 cohort of students undertook a similar digital assignment and follow-up survey, and while not used extensively in this discussion, some quotes from 2007 are used within this chapter to illustrate the continuity of issues across cohorts.

**Table 8.1**   Student course evaluations

| Total enrolment | 176 |
| --- | --- |
| Responses to Course Evaluation Instrument | 92 |
| Optional responses to Qs 11 and 12 | 85 |
| Digital portrait referred to response to Q11 (strengths of the course) | 42 |
| Digital portrait referred to response to Q12 (ways course could be improved) | 30 |
| Comments categorized as foregrounding a particular element of the multiliteracies pedagogy: | 67 |
| Situated practice | 17 |
| Overt instruction | 14 |
| Critical framing | 18 |
| Transformed practice | 18 |

All text responses that alluded to the digital portrait within questions 11 and 12 have been mapped in an attempt to develop a comprehensive and instructive understanding of the experiences of the student-teachers in relation to that task. These student-teacher evaluations of the digital portrait as an assessment item have been read through the lens of the four elements of the multiliteracies framework – *situated learning, overt instruction, critical framing* and *transformed practice* – and the discussion below describes and addresses each of these dimensions in turn. There is inevitable overlap where, for example, a comment on the situatedness of the task connects also to overt learning, and in such cases a judgement has been made, for the sake of clarity and inclusion, to categorize that statement within the element that appears to be foregrounded by the student-teacher. It is interesting to note the apparent balance across the four dimensions within student-teacher responses, perhaps indicating the relevance of the multiliteracies pedagogy to this particular analysis.

## Situated learning

Cope and Kalantzis (2000) describe situated learning as that 'aspect of the curriculum [that] needs to recruit learners' previous and current experiences, as well as their extra-school communities and discourses, as an integral part of the learning experience' (p. 33). Within the context of the digital portrait assignment, this element is most evident in the connections student-teachers make to their own learning within the university as well as their future professional roles as educators, and comments are drawn out that demonstrate the effectiveness or otherwise of our attempts as teacher educators to situate their learning and construction of the digital portraits. Many of the comments from students alluded to a strong connection between this assignment and its relevance to their work with young people in schools:

> The way that literacy and its varying forms were approached were fantastic. I have a greater understanding of the many different ways I can approach literacy within the classroom situation ... the digital portrait was a fantastic assignment to do in place of an essay, but it was much more time-consuming than the written work.

> [There was] genuine interest in developing future literacy educators; developing ICT skills by making them part of the assessment.

> I think it is great that this course gives us the chance to learn and use technology in a way that can be used with our students.

These responses suggest a pragmatic approach where skills learned can be transferred from academic to professional settings, as well as an appreciation of changing theoretical understandings of what constitutes literacy teaching and learning. These students imagine themselves replicating the process, with simpler texts, within a classroom setting, in ways that are not possible with a traditional academic essay.

Not all students agreed, however, and there were several students whose views were picked up a year later by one student in the 2007 cohort who felt that 'fanciful ideas about digital literacies' (2007 CEI feedback) were too dominant within the course:

> I did not feel that I was learning anything that was going to assist me as a teacher through the assignments. They were actually detracting from the real life issues and schooling and provided no depth into how to teach children literacy ...

Another student in 2007 failed to find any connection between the digital requirements at university and the reality of the classroom he or she worked in during practicum:

> Prac revealed that literacy concerns in classrooms do not go beyond spelling and recounts ... we should be given info concerning genres of written work.

However, it was not only what students encountered on practicum that influenced them, but also reactionary media and community responses to anything seen to detract from traditional print literacies. One student claimed that 'students need basic skills first' before they can engage in critical and/or digital literacies, and such assertions suggest a disjuncture between the student's experiences of literacy teaching and learning and the theoretical perspectives covered in the course that conceive of 'basic skills' as embedded within and integral to critical and digital literacies (Kerin and Nixon, 2005).

The comments from students suggest that successful integration of digital literacies needs to be carefully balanced with traditional literacies to enable student-teachers to not only recognize connections and relevance to classrooms, but also to address the politics of literacy that student-teachers bring with them to university and are faced with anew in the media and debates about education. Rather than discount discourses of mandated assessment or performativity, or assume that student-teachers will appreciate the need to become digitally literate themselves, new learning and theories relating to digital literacies must first be situated within the familiar and often uncharted literacy landscape of student-teachers.

## Overt instruction

In addition to the exploration and discussion of key theoretical concepts, such as Moll et al.'s (1992) funds of knowledge and Thomson's (2002) virtual school-bag, that were at the heart of the student-teachers' examination of a child/adolescent's in- and out-of-school literacies, provision was made for overt instruction, described as:

> collaborative efforts between teacher and student wherein the student is both allowed to accomplish a task more complex than they can establish on their own, and where they come to conscious awareness of the teacher's representation and interpretation of the task and its relations to other aspects of what is being learned. (Cope and Kalantzis, 2000, p. 33)

Accordingly, a range of opportunities were provided for students to master PowerPoint, and to consider their interpretation and response in relation to this particular task. This included three voluntary workshops scheduled in computer laboratories for group and one-on-one support for students to learn how to construct a PowerPoint and critique individual digital portraits in progress. In addition, hyperlinks to online PowerPoint tutorials were added into online materials, brief demonstrations and advice were provided during lectures and tutorials, and a work in progress was modelled across a series of lectures and posted to the course homepage.

Despite an overwhelming impression, during the period of construction of the assignment, that many students were floundering and felt under-resourced and under-supported to successfully construct their assignment, the formal evaluations suggest otherwise, and there was an even balance of comments across question 11 (strengths of the course) and question 12 (weaknesses of the course). Of those who were critical in relation to overt instruction, comments tended to focus on the perceived lack clarity of the assignment and the need for more direct technical support:

> More assistance could have been given: what a distinction or pass (PS) would look like.

> Assignment 2 needed more prep going into it. It was a bit like being thrown in the deep end … difficulty understanding what was expected of us.

What appeared to be the most strongly expressed sentiment rejected the notion that the development of digital literacies was at all relevant to such a course:

> Remove the digital aspect from assignment: I wasted far too many hours on the 'technical' aspect of the assignments when I really needed to focus on content. If it was so necessary for us to do a 'technical assignment' then a computing course should be added to the program.

Clearly the student is not rejecting the content of the assignment, but would appear to oppose both the multimodality of the assignment and the theoretical concepts that were integral to the course, separating as he or she does the technical, conceptual, and communicative literacies inherent in the task.

In contrast to these comments, a number of students commented on the usefulness of a model and explicit instruction:

> (It) provided a strong sense of what was expected.

> The example of the digital profile was very helpful as was the reference to assignments in lectures.

> (It) was taught with enthusiasm … the teacher knew her stuff and was confident in teaching it.

> The outline was well written which ultimately made it easier and clearer to meet the requirements.

Such comments suggest that the construction and modelling of the assignment by the teacher educator was significant, and that students require both theoretical and technical input and guidance, particularly when the task diverts from more familiar academic exercises undertaken at university. An awareness that not all students are expert or confident with digital technologies, and that they require the support of teachers with relevant expertise, is fundamental not only to overt instruction but also impacts on critical framing discussed below.

## Critical framing

Within the Multiliteracies framework, the critical dimension is intended to 'help learners frame their growing mastery in practice (Situated Practice) and conscious control and understanding (Overt Instruction) in relation to the historical, social, cultural, political, ideological, and value-centred relations of particular systems of knowledge and social practice' (Cope and Kalantzis, 2000, p. 34). There is no doubt that in the context of schooling, critical examination of relationships, knowledge and practices are vital (Comber and Simpson, 2001) and, in relation to digital literacies, this is very often associated with issues of access to or exclusion from resources, including hardware, software and connectivity to the internet (Nixon, 2001):

> Consideration needed for people who do not have the latest and greatest technology at home (e.g. microphones, Microsoft Office and headphones).

> The emphasis on ICTs (Information Communications Technologies) was excessive, and the second assignment was massive – way too much given the weighting.

Criticisms of the course persisted in relation to inaccessibility to hardware and software, despite the decision by the teaching team to use an application like PowerPoint precisely because it is so widely available. Some issues arose because students had pirated versions of Windows on home computers, while other students had found it difficult to borrow microphones, headphones or cameras. At least one student had no computer at home and was forced to purchase a USB flashdrive when he realized that the floppy disk he brought into one of the workshops was no longer usable on university computers. The technical aspects were particularly challenging for this student and others, yet the context of working with children and adolescents in schools suggests that engagement with digital literacies in their university degree is of particular significance for those students with limited experience or access at home.

Some students believed that this assignment, more than any others they had undertaken, created injustice because of the diverse expertise and experience with digital technologies across the cohort:

> It also unfairly privileged some students and disadvantaged others (because of access to ICTs).

> ICT component could be stressed prior to enrolling to allow the less knowledgeable in this area to take courses in this area to bring skills on a par with peers.

This view was reiterated in discussions with students who assumed that students come to oral and written assessment tasks with equitable resources and knowledge, and such exchanges productively engage student-teachers in conversations that denaturalize and make strange their familiar practices and discourses. One of the students believed that the digital assignment provided opportunities for some students to enhance the communication of their learning in ways that were not possible in oral or print language:

> The variety of assignments has been great ... the scope for all students to be given the opportunity to excel.

Another student acknowledged that despite her reluctance, she benefited from being forced out of her comfort zone in traditional assignments:

> Although I didn't like the ICT assignments I did appreciate why we did them. I am more ICT literate than before and I thank the course for that.

And although the student does not say why she appreciated being more ICT literate, it might be assumed that she understands the advantages of developing such skills for future professional relationships and contexts.

## Transformed practice

Within the Multiliteracies framework, Transformed Practice demands that learners 're-create a discourse by engaging in it for [our own] real purposes' (Cope and Kalantzis, 2000, p. 36). In a university context, quite often the purpose for textual production is to satisfy criteria identified by teaching staff rather than for students' real purposes, though attempts may be made to build relevance for learners. In this brief discussion of student perceptions of, and responses to, Transformed Practice in relation to the digital portrait, the focus is on the mobilization of new knowledge and technical skills rather than on the assignment generally, because broader aspects of assessment have been covered previously in this discussion. All 17 comments categorized as Transformed Practice were made by students in response to question 11 where they were asked to identify strengths of the course. These comments focused on the advantages of being able to communicate their knowledge in new ways:

> The ability to integrate multiple way of demonstrating our knowledge in assignments.

> Keep with Assignment 2: it was challenging but a great experience.

> Integration of alternative assessment tasks further enhanced my skills which will help me in the workplace. It was refreshing and rewarding to be assessed by another form in contrast to essays alone.

> Really excellent in terms of pushing students to explore the many different literacies ... forced students to learn new skills.

> The digital portrait assignment is brilliant. It allowed us to interact with the student on a professional but fun environment. It allowed us to pursue our learning in a real life situation ...

While many comments focused on what might be conceived as the novelty value of such an assignment, other comments do recognize the active learning that took place in the construction of the text, through references to the 'hands-on' element or of being 'pushed' or 'forced' or allowed to 'pursue' new learning in the process. It is curious to see that student-teachers regarded the additional pressure inherent in the assignment as a strength of the course, and this is consistent with the claim that multiliteracies pedagogy supports learners to be 'ideally creative and responsible makers of meaning' (Cope and Kalantzis, 2000, p. 36). This is not to suggest that a print assignment or traditional essay does not facilitate such agency, but the claim is made here that it was the multimodality and strangeness of the assignment within their university context that led the majority of students to make creative responses, and for so many of them to signal deeper, more engaged learning than was their usual experience.

## Students-teachers as multiliterate learners and educators

This analysis explores the responses of student-teachers to an assignment that led them to examine the cultural and linguistic diversity of a child/adolescent and the implications of such diversity for literacy teaching and learning, and to represent that new knowledge in a multimodal text. The multiliteracies pedagogy has enabled a systematic and productive analysis of student-teacher responses across four dimensions, and reveals a range of insights and implications for teacher education. First, student-teachers do not necessarily accept theoretical positions that address the emergence of new digital technologies and literacies, and teacher educators must situate their own teaching to take account of diverse political positions in relation to changing literacies, and provide compelling evidence and research to validate the inclusion of digital literacies in university courses. Secondly, teacher educators, like classroom teachers, cannot assume universal digital competence, engagement, or excitement. Provision of clear expectations and models, coupled with explicit teaching and one-on-one support, are as necessary with digital literacies as with traditional print assignments, and this demands that teacher educators develop their own skills and capacities as designers and producers of digital texts. Thirdly, issues of access and equity are vitally important. Rather than replicate generations of disadvantage, all prospective educators, and especially those who come from or will teach within disadvantaged communities where access to digital technologies and connectivity may be problematic, must attract particular attention and consideration. The goal should be to provide those emerging educators with enhanced knowledge and experience to enable them to participate in a regeneration of literacy teaching that takes account of the two 'multis' referred to at the beginning of this article: multimodality and multiple ways of being and acting in the world. Finally, student responses suggest that this assignment was more demanding and challenging than they had imagined, but that their investment of intellect and time was well rewarded.

While the assignment discussed here is not interactive, does not take advantage of Web 2.0 technologies and uses a ubiquitous application that will soon be redundant, student-teacher evaluations suggest that for some the task was extremely challenging. For some it was a 'brilliant exercise', while another student made just one comment: 'Get rid of the digital assignment!' The assignment highlighted the 'digital schism' that lies between those with extensive access to, experience and confidence with digital technologies, and those with limited access and experience, or dispositions that act as barriers to learning with digital technologies. Just as we educate our student-teachers to be critical, inclusive educators, we must also challenge and provide opportunities for them to extend simultaneously their theoretical understandings of digital literacies and competence with digital technologies so that they can in turn address the divide that persists in many school classrooms.

> If our new and intending primary school teachers are making a separation between their own assets with new media and the way that such media might play a part in education, then there is a serious risk of a continued and widening schism between the work of the school and the world of life outside. (Robinson and Mackey, 2006, p. 213)

It may be that the effects of such assignments do not materialize until after student-teachers graduate and engage with the realities of educating young people. While drafting this chapter, I received an email from one of these 2006 students who suffered extreme frustration at the time because of her very limited experience with digital technologies. She now teaches young men who are particularly vulnerable and disadvantaged, and over the space of two years has extended her PowerPoint skills to movie-making.

> You will be pleased to know that movie maker is still doing big business (here). Just this week one of my boys who is at about grade 2 reading and less than that for writing, entered a movie maker project on Hep C in an external competition. He did a really good job. He took the skills we had used in intensive literacy with Movie Maker and applied them in his SOSE (Studies of Society and Environment) class which was a big step for him. The digital assignment was still one of the most useful things we did at uni! (Email correspondence)

This does not suggest that digital assignments are a panacea. However, it does challenge all educators to engage with digital possibilities, even while we attempt to breach the uncertainty, frustration and limitations of our experience and conceptual knowledge as we undertake such endeavours.

# References

Alvermann, D.E., Hinchman, K.A., Moore, D.W., Phelps, S.F. and Waff, D.R. (2006) *Reconceptualizing the Literacies in Adolescents' Lives.* 2nd edn. Mahwah, NJ: Lawrence Erlbaum Associates.

Buckingham, D. (2003) *Media Education: Literacy, Learning and Contemporary Culture.* Cambridge: Polity.

Carrington, V. (2006) *Rethinking Middle Years: Early Adolescents, Schooling and Digital Culture.* Crows' Nest, NSW: Allen & Unwin.

Comber, B. and Simpson, A. (eds) (2001) *Negotiating Critical Literacies in Classrooms.* Mahwah, NJ: Lawrence Erlbaum Associates.

Cope, B. and Kalantzis, M. (eds) (2000) *Multiliteracies: Literacy Learning and the Design of Social Futures.* London: Macmillan.

Doherty, C. (2007) 'Masterclass pedagogy for multimedia applications in teacher education', *Teaching Education*, 18(4): 313–27.

Durrant, C. and Beavis, C. (eds) (2001) *P(ICT)ures of English: Teachers, Learners and Technology.* Adelaide: Wakefield Press.

Evans, J. (ed.) (2005) *Literacy Moves On: Popular Culture, New Technologies and Critical Literacy in the Elementary Classroom.* Portsmouth, NH: Heinemann.

Gee, J.P. (2003) *What Video Games Have to Teach Us about Learning and Literacy.* New York: Palgrave Macmillan.

Graham, L. (2008) 'Teachers are digikids too: the digital histories and digital lives of young teachers in English primary schools', *Literacy*, 42(1): 10–18.

Jewitt, C. and Kress, G. (2003) *Multimodal Literacy.* New York: Peter Lang.

Kerin, R. and Nixon, H. (2005) 'Middle years English/literacy curriculum: the interface of critical literacy and digital texts', *Literacy Learning: The Middle Years*, 13(1): 20–35.

Kist, W. (2005) *New Literacies in Action: Teaching and Learning in Multiple Media.* New York and London: Teachers College Press.

Kress, G. (2000) 'A curriculum for the future', *Cambridge Journal of Education*, 30(1): 133–45.

Kress, G. (2003) *Literacy in the New Media Age.* London and New York: Routledge.

Krumsvik, R. (2006) 'The digital challenges of school and teacher education in Norway: some urgent questions and the search for answers', *Education Information Technology*, 11: 239–56.

Lankshear, C. and Knobel, M. (2003) *New Literacies: Changing Knowledge and Classroom Learning.* Buckingham and Philadelphia, PA: Open University Press.

Loveless, A., Burton, J. and Turvey, K. (2006) 'Developing conceptual frameworks for creativity, ICT and teacher education', *Thinking Skills and Creativity*, 1: 3–13.

Marsh, J. and Millard, E. (eds) (2006) *Popular Literacies, Childhood and Schooling.* London and New York: Routledge.

Moll, L., Amanti, C., Neff, D. and Gonzalez, N. (1992) 'Funds of knowledge for teaching: using a qualitative approach to connect homes and classrooms', *Theory into Practice*, 31(2): 132–41.

New London Group (1996) 'A pedagogy of multiliteracies: designing social futures', *Harvard Education Review*, 66(1): 60–92.

Nixon, H. (2001) 'Literacy, ICTs and disadvantage: an "unspeakable" topic?', in C. Durrant and C. Beavis (eds), *P(ICT)ures of English*. Adelaide: AATE/Wakefield Press. pp. 191–209.

Robinson, M. and Mackey, M. (2006) 'Assets in the classroom: comfort and competence with media among teachers past and present', in J. Marsh and E. Millard (eds), *Popular Literacies, Childhood and Schooling*. London and New York: Routledge. pp. 200–20.

Thomson, P. (2002) *Schooling the Rustbelt Kids: Making a Difference in Changing Times.* Crows' Nest, NSW: Allen & Unwin.

# Download

## Key points

1. Literacy teachers and teacher-educators must develop their own flexible and expanding digital literacies to support classroom integration of such literacies.
2. Literacy teachers and teacher-educators must allow for a diversity of experience, interest in and disposition to digital technologies across any cohort of learners, and provide modelling of textual design and construction as well as explicit teaching and timely intervention.
3. Literacy teachers and teacher-educators must engage in the ongoing development of their own knowledge and expertise in both traditional and digital literacies to enable them to participate knowledgeably and critically in debates about what constitutes literacy teaching and learning in the twenty-first century.

## In your classroom

1. Value and model the distinctive and overlapping contributions and power of both traditional and digital literacies.
2. Be prepared to demonstrate with your learners the design, construction and critique of your own digital texts that will serve as models for your students.
3. Mandate digital assessments and support all students to achieve, particularly those with no or limited access beyond school, or those disinclined to engage with digital technologies.

## Further reading

Evans, J. (ed.) (2005) *Literacy Moves On: Popular Culture, New Technologies and Critical Literacy in the Elementary Classroom*. Portsmouth, NH: Heinemann.

Kist, W. (2005) *New Literacies in Action: Teaching and Learning in Multiple Media*. New York and London: Teachers College Press.

Lankshear, C. and Knobel, M. (2003) *New Literacies: Changing Knowledge and Classroom Learning*. Buckingham and Philadelphia, PA: Open University Press.

# Composing with Old and
# New Media: Toward a Parallel
# Pedagogy

*Kevin Leander*

## Introduction

When it comes to popular social practices with visual texts among youth, including video gaming, web surfing, and now, uploading short films and television shows to video iPods, it is often unclear to educators what stance we might take (Bruce, 1997). Are such practices a distraction to literacy education, or are they a part of literacy itself? Even if visuals are important, how can we possibly fit more into an already overcrowded curriculum, even if we do decide to buy into an expanded definition of what it means to be literate (Kinzer and Leander, 2003)? Behind such questions is a key issue with important consequences: how do we imagine the relationship of so-called 'new literacies' (Lankshear and Knobel, 2003) to more conventional print-based literacies? In broad strokes, we can describe four common stances on this relationship that are part of our current teaching and research imaginations: resistance, replacement, return and remediation.

The 'resistance' stance involves taking a position squarely with conventional print literacy practices, including reading, interpreting and writing print genres that have been valued in (and out) of school for generations, such as the novel, the academic argument, poetry, the research paper and the like. A stance of resistance may well not be conservation for conservation's sake (as in the innovation curmudgeon or technophobe) but may be a practical response to increased pressure from standards movements to make sure that all children are well educated in conventional literacy practices. Resisters see new literacies, including visual practices, as interfering in the difficult and increasingly assessed business of print literacy practices.

The 'replacement' stance is quite the opposite of that of resistance. Teachers and researchers taking this stance point out the outdatedness and irrelevance of much of what school teaches as literacy. The novel, the academic argument, the poem and the research paper are dead genres, and should be substituted with genres more likely to be found in the native, everyday practices of youth. Film analysis might replace novel interpretation, multimedia persuasion through websites may be a more appropriate set of skills for the future workplace than the academic argument, and the aesthetics of poetry writing and analysis may be better updated by engaging the aesthetics of weblogs. Educators with a replacement stance are often the technophilic counterparts to the technophobia of resisters. In fact, these two stances can serve to perpetuate one another, acting as foils for one another's position.

A common stance that lies somewhere between resistance and replacement may be described as 'return'. By return I mean to indicate a stance that values new literacy practices but validates and defends them with respect to print. The return stance, therefore, is essentially printcentric. Film interpretation or film production is a valued set of activities, but this valuing is primarily measured by how the analysis of still images, moving images, soundtracks and the like scaffold the interpretation and production of conventional literature. In pedagogical practice, new media productions and interpretations do not stand on their own. Rather, new literacy engagements often conclude with print. For instance, if students produce a multimedia project of some type, the project is accompanied by print commentary about what it means and/or about what the composer was thinking while producing it (critiqued by Kist, 2005). This final print piece is considered as a key means of interpreting the value of multi-media engagement.

A final stance may be labelled as 'remediation', which is an imperfect label to indicate not a remedial programme for struggling students, but rather the way in which the meanings and effects of familiar texts and textual forms are communicated, or mediated once again, through less familiar textual forms (Bolter and Grusin, 1999). Relatively 'new' semiotic forms, including the increasing use of visuals in everyday communication, do not abandon old forms, but rather include and embed their generic conventions, structures and practices in new ways. In sum, the new is never entirely apart from the old. A second meaning of the remediation stance for literacy pedagogy is that we are currently in need of understanding the modes of thinking and learning that we want our students to engage in, and consider which media, including print, still and moving images, music, voice, embodied performance, or other that might best 'mediate' such modes of thinking and learning. A remediation stance, therefore, sees different media as neither interfering with one another (as in the resistance stance) nor replacing one another. Moreover, no single means of media (print, visuals or other) assumes a central position in this stance (as in the return stance); the person taking a remediation stance is agnostic with respect to the existence of any supreme media. The creation of meanings and effects upon audiences is of central concern, as are processes of production and interpretation that presume that multimedia is not exceptional, but actually more typical than mono-media.

In this chapter, I assume a stance of remediation as I describe an approach to 'parallel pedagogy' that I am developing in a composition course. Parallel pedagogy is a way of describing how old and new literacy practices, including print texts and visual texts, may be fruitfully taught side by side, rather than the 'old' being a precursor to the new or being replaced by it. In a master's-level composition course, students (pre-service teachers) compose conventional print memoir pieces and they compose digital stories. These digital stories are multimedia compositions that play as short films, and typically involve still images, music tracks, video clips, voice tracks, visual transitions and visual effects. My purpose in having students compose with various media is to expand their conceptual understanding of composition and their practical, working knowledge of different semiotic resources and systems. I strive with my students to build a common meta-level language or grammar of storytelling (memoir) that is functional and valuable across media. Regardless of the media used, for example, storytellers are concerned with conveying some sort of 'big idea' to their audience, and in the course we use language such as 'big idea' and other terms to discuss the possibilities and challenges of composition in different media.

At the same time, in this course we also analyse, discuss and work out ways practically in which different media have different affordances (Gibson, 1979), or ways of functioning that allow them very different potentials to create effects and make meanings. While a print memoir, for instance, might convey a big idea through a repeated key phrase, a photograph might convey its big idea through the way in which the subject is visually framed, or via the angle that the viewer is given with respect to the image subject (Kress and van Leeuwen, 1996). While 'big idea' provides us with a common language, this dimension of storytelling may be worked out in very different ways in distinct media. Moreover, these issues get all the more complex when multiple media are playing at the same time as one another, in different simultaneous tracks of a composition, as in the case of digital storytelling.

In what follows, the discussion of parallel pedagogy proceeds in two main sections. First, I offer a broad overview of the composition course, expanding on the introduction given thus far. Second, I discuss specific course activities that are structured to scaffold students' understandings of how visuals, in story composition, may be understood through a set of dimensions that also relate to print and other media. In the final part of the second section, I focus on one student's project to offer a more detailed view of how parallel pedagogy functions and the kinds of thinking and learning it fosters.

## Overview of 'Teaching composition by traversing "old" and "new" media'

'Teaching composition' is a composition pedagogy course offered to master's students at Vanderbilt who are preparing to teach English at the secondary school level. The course approaches the activity of composing with 'an expanded tool kit' (Smagorinski, 2002) that includes, but is not limited to, print. The course is created to value and scaffold students' understandings of print composition without limiting the notion of composing to print media; the fact that we use 'compose' and 'composition' to describe the activity and products of writers, visual artists and sculptors alike is taken as an invitation to explore how composing shares something in common across media. This approach to common dimensions across media is framed, in relation to the personal memoir, by examining several 'dimensions' of composition that are relevant across diverse media. For example, within print memoirs, voice may be defined as the 'speaking personality' of the writer (Bakhtin, 1986). Yet, in composing and arranging photographs or other visual texts, we also recognize something akin to the personality of the composer – her or his persona communicating through the images. In this manner, we may also discuss the 'voice' of the photographer. In considering a music or recorded voice track, by contrast, we might consider material qualities of voice that are not easily afforded by print or visuals, including timbre, resonance and pitch. Hence, the notion of 'voice' remains highly meaningful across media. These kinds of considerations and comparisons are key to what I intend by developing a parallel pedagogy. Other dimensions considered include transition, focus or 'big idea', place and time, and others.

Students in 'Teaching composition' create a multimedia digital story as a final class project that is five to ten minutes in length, and is based on earlier versions of a print memoir that they have written. We use (Apple) iMovie in this project as the learning curve with iMovie is not steep. Final stories are presented in a Digital Story Film Festival at the end of the semester. Along with this product- and audience-focus of the course, students are assigned a number of in-progress composition assignments, including two different written memoirs, an image memoir piece, a storyboard and others. These assignments draw on and juxtapose different media, including print but also sound voice recordings and images. Thus, a large degree of process work in both print and non-print media precedes the final production of the digital story. Additionally, these pieces are produced through peer response and revising groups, a process that is familiar within writing-process pedagogies (for example, Atwell, 1998). Many students who have taken the course have reported that one of its major effects on them was to be convinced of the importance of response and revision during the composing process. It appears that there is a particular visual and material relationship provided by working on multimedia that makes the idea of revision and response more immediately and powerfully visible than working in print alone. For example, in the multimedia workshop environment, students share pictures, music tracks and tips for creating particular effects for others' projects to a degree that I have not experienced when students respond to print texts alone

## Parallel pedagogy with pictures

The three following examples are of specific lessons and activities intended to juxtapose the interpretation and creation of images with that of print texts.

These examples of parallel pedagogy, drawn from 'Teaching composition', are intended here to suggest a pedagogical orientation from which a broad range of lessons and learning experiences could be developed.

## Analysis of big idea in print and digital stories

Roorbach (1998, p. 55) notes that the big idea of a written piece is a broader notion than the notion of thesis; the idea is the 'underlying conception or conceptions that give a piece of successful writing its unity – the kind of unity that plot sometimes brings to fiction'. As a writing teacher, it has often surprised me how difficult it is for students to learn the related notions of 'guiding idea,' 'big idea,' or 'thesis'. It seems as if second graders through to adult writers struggle with the same problem in different texts. In memoir-writing at the secondary school level, I've often noticed how some of my students seem to catch on quickly to the subtle ways in which a skilled writer makes the underlying conception of her memoir come to life, while other students seem to write personal essays or memoirs that either lack a central conception or have it mercilessly tagged on ('And that's when I learned that it always pays to be prepared.'). Throughout the entire process of working on print memoirs and digital stories, we talk a great deal about the notion of 'big idea', but early on in the process we also deliberately analyse memoir pieces in print and other pieces as digital stories to make explicit comparisons about how their big ideas are conveyed. In the following, I give a sense of this activity by drawing on one student's observational notes and comparisons.

A print memoir piece that I like to use is the story 'Adjustments', by Jeanne Brinkman Grinnan (Kitchen and Jones, 1999). 'Adjustments' is a lovely, haunting piece that is just over a page in length, a kind of still life of a mother setting and winding the house clocks as her daughter looks on. Nothing happens in the story, which is made meaningful by how the event it shot through with the narrator's memories of the father, who took on this task himself along with other activities requiring his meticulous attention. The clock-setting calls up themes of time being marked and passing in the midst of loss, just as the mother's position atop a chair, as she winds the clocks, calls up themes of balance at risk. 'Kate', a student in my class, wrote the following observational notes about how the big idea of 'Adjustments' was conveyed:

> Clocks (uncaptured time) metaphor/physical symbol for something bigger than self; details connect to themes.
> Example: falling mother, changing clock, taking out trash.
> Repetition.

One of the digital stories that I use for conveying the dimension of big idea is 'BJ's Story', from the website Silence Speaks (www.silencespeaks.org). Like the other stories at this site, 'BJ's Story' is a story about experiencing violence, in this case, through the words of a boy observing his alcoholic father continually abusing his mother. The story is told in poetic form, with a rap rhythm, and the visuals move across photos, abstract art and symbolic images. Kate's observational notes on the big idea in 'BJ's Story' were as follows:

> Zoom and camera focus/out of focus
> Hand in chains, repeated images
> Repeated beat – idea carried on
> Flashback to kid and kid's eyes
> 'All I could do was watch her hands.'
> 'Internally bleed' – language is poignant.
> Coupling of religious images/plaster/violence.

After comparing several print and multimedia stories, I asked the students to synthesize their thoughts about how 'big idea' functions in similar and different ways in print and non-print. Kate drew out some thoughtful initial comparisons in this activity. Among them, she noted that both print and digital stories 'pay attention to details as a way of showing main ideas'. Kate especially noted that 'deliberate and purposeful' word choice in both forms of storytelling was essential to shaping the big idea. Additionally, she pointed out that print and visual texts function with repetitions of certain figures, and pointed out as an example the clocks in 'Adjustments' and images of hands (for abuse) within 'BJ's Story'. In terms of differences, or the specific affordances of print versus multimedia storytelling, Kate remarked that the relations among the music and images and soundtrack, in digital stories, serve to establish the main idea, and offered as an example the steady rhythmic beat that gave a pulsing, menacing background tone to 'BJ's Story'. While Kate noticed that different media might work together in the digital stories, she also made an important observation that media may move in different directions: 'digital (media) can show irony through juxtaposition of "mismatched" pictures, music, words, etc.' By contrast, a special affordance that Kate remarked about print media was that it could present a less distracting main idea; while media could work together (or intentionally apart), multiple media tracks could also just simply be distracting if not produced well.

In class, we often used this broad type of observation, inquiry and synthesis activity to consider how different dimensions of composition are realized in print and non-print texts (digital stories, film, still images, comic strips, and so on). Of course, the variation among stories within any particular media (for example, print stories as a category) may also be very great; we cannot make easy claims about how just a few stories stand for an entire media type. However, by looking closely, comparing, synthesizing and filtering one's thinking through a key dimension such as 'big idea', students begin to develop ways of looking and analysing that could readily lead to and motivate more detailed or technical analyses.

## Transition workshop: verbal and visual grammars

The transition workshop is relatively simply structured as an inquiry into the functions and differences among linguistic and visual transitions. I begin this workshop with a discussion of common linguistic transitions and transitional phrases in print texts and their various functions, using a list such as that offered by the Department of Rhetoric and Composition at Oberlin College (www.oberlin.edu/rhetoric/writing/assist/paragraphs.html), excerpted below:

- To show cause and effect: therefore, thus, consequently, as a result, for this reason, so, so that
- To compare: however, on the one hand/on the other hand, in contrast, conversely, but, yet, nevertheless, nonetheless, on the contrary, still
- To show addition: and, in addition, also, furthermore, moreover, besides
- To indicate time: before, now, after, afterwards, subsequently, later, earlier, meanwhile, in the meantime, while, as long as, so far.

Of course, the skill of creating effective transitions in print cannot be limited to learning a list of terms; we also discuss other means of transitioning between sentences and paragraphs, including referring to old information, repeating key words and providing top-level language and headings so that readers can make their way through long pieces.

After discussing linguistic transitions, and looking specifically at their use within different stories and other print texts, I ask the students to view the transitions provided by iMovie, which are a subset of a much larger group of transitions used in film, and to describe the meaning that they believe each transition has. The transitions used in a recent version of iMovie included billow, circle closing, circle opening, cross dissolve, fade in, overlap, push, radial, ripple and several others. Filmic transitions are difficult to represent as still images, but the images in Figures 9.1, 9.2 and 9.3 suggest something of the range of what students would be seeing in iMovie.

**Figure 9.1** Circle closing transition

**Figure 9.2** Cross dissolve transition

**Figure 9.3** Push transition

As they view these various transitions, the students fill in a chart that offers verbal equivalents of the meanings of these visuals. For example, in an excerpt of
one student's work (Table 9.1), she indicated that cross dissolve carried a meaning of cause and effect, such as is conveyed by the word 'consequently', and, by
contrast, that the push transition indicated time moving forward, such as in

the word 'subsequently', or perhaps simultaneity with a right to left push. Other students had different ideas, worthy of comparison and discussion. My concern in this activity is not that students identify a single correct (verbal) meaning for (visual) film transitions. In fact, it is certain that some visual transitions have no verbal equivalent at all, and that movement in the opposite direction is also incomplete. Rather, my key goal is that students develop a meta-level approach to considering how transitions are a dimension that composers in print and film routinely address, and that the functions of transitions in expressing relations among ideas, movements in space and time, causes and effects, comparisons and other relations are functions that traverse media. In order to push students' parallel thinking about transitions, I ask them, alone or in pairs, to write a short paragraph comparing verbal and visual transitions, based upon their enquiry. In the following, one student begins to suggest his understanding of visual transitions as having unique meanings:

Table 9.1 Student comparisons of visual and verbal (print) transitions

| iMovie | Print text (student responses) |
| --- | --- |
| Billow | To give example, to illustrate, for example |
| Circle closing | To emphasize a point: in fact |
| Circle opening | To conclude or summarize, in summary |
| Cross dissolve | Cause & effect, consequently |
| Fade in | To introduce; at first |
| Overlap | To show cause & effect; for this reason; as a result |
| Push | To indicate time: subsequently, meanwhile (depends on which way you push) |

> In iMovie, different transitions have distinct implications: a push, for instance, a different relationship than a cross-dissolve, just as the expressions 'instead of' and 'however' evoke different relationships in print. Across media, transitions connect ideas, show relationships and heighten the drama. Equivalencies or connections seem to exist across media.

At the same time that this student noted similar transition functions across media, in his analysis he also argued that print offered a greater range of 'specific and subtle' transitions than film: 'For example, are there equivalent transitional devices like "nonetheless" and "furthermore" in non-print domains?' This type of response gave us the opportunity to discuss how print may have greater affordances for certain kinds of logical connections, while film has unique and unusual affordances for space–time relationships. Moreover, discussion based on these initial analyses readily turns to the simultaneity of transitions across different media tracks within film – where, for instance, a music track, rhythm or voice-over may continue while visuals shift (or vice versa). Further, a number of students noted how the meanings of visual transitions were highly dependent upon the particulars of the visuals themselves. Had I picked up on this insight earlier, it could have provided a productive basis for a conversation on how visual and verbal transitions depend on the immediate texts-in-use for their meanings.

## Storyboarding: a rich space for parallel pedagogy

One way of seeing the activity of storyboarding is simply that a storyboard is the organization of material that is already gathered. Storyboarding, in this view, is to a visual story what outlining is to a print story – a parallel sequence of images, voiceover text, notes on the soundtrack, transitions and effects, somewhat akin to a comic strip (Lambert, 2002; and Figures 9.4, 9.5 and 9.6). However, stressing the organizational aspects of storyboarding can risk under-estimating the ways in which storyboarding can be an important means of generating new media, and learning dimensions of composition that traverse media types. As students moved from print memoir drafts to storyboarding and finally to their digital stories, a number of important transformations occurred, which pushed them to consider what media they wanted to carry the informa-tion load at any point in their developing stories and prompted them to consider the complex relationships of either sequential or simultaneous media. Following, I give a brief sampling of one student's ('Todd's') progression through these stages.

### Focusing the big idea through the image

An early draft of Todd's print memoir began with two paragraphs that were somewhat conventional in introductory style. Todd started out with a broad introduction to the idea of bad luck during travel, made reference to a past trip to Europe, and finally took the reader to the very beginning of a more recent trip to San Francisco and his trepidations of what might happen. Using this writing as a base for his digital story, Todd confronted the problem of economy. These first two original paragraphs, 228 words in length, would take up too much time. This temporal constraint pushed Todd to reconsider what the big idea of his story is, and how much of this original print text would be neces-sary for it. Second, it pushed him to think about how to re-mediate some of this verbal text into other media. Todd eventually cut his written memoir in half as he transformed it into a digital story, a process that he reported as 'sometimes painful'. In the following reflection on his project, Todd writes how peer and professor responses shaped the eventual digital story.

> When it was mentioned that I might really be writing about life's possibilities, I admitted that kind of an idea had been floating around in my head lately and could have influenced the writing of my print memoir unintentionally. I decided to make my almost unconscious thoughts about possibility more explicit in the story by removing my initial introduction and conclusion, which focused on notions of home and travel, and by calling more attention to my thoughts upon leaving the [Gay Pride] parade, when I was faced with so many possibilities of what my life could become. I then decided to use Leona Naess' song 'Calling' ... to contribute to this 'possibilities' theme and began to consider the parade as a symbol of that which is possible in my life.

In the first frames of Todd's storyboard (Figures 9.4, 9.5 and 9.6), this transformation of the big idea of his story towards the possibilities of life is evident, and the 'possibilities' theme becomes remediated through parade images, which now not only began the story but also permeate it throughout.

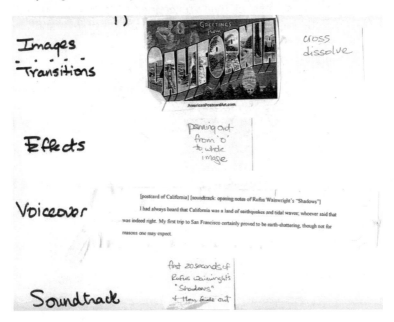

**Figure 9.4**  Todd's storyboard, frame 1

*Adding meaning through photographic perspective*

As Todd thinks visually and photographically, he also draws on the ways in which a photographer assumes a perspective on her or his subject, and how this perspective itself conveys meaning. He focuses in particular on the high angle from which the parade was shot (Figure 9.5), and how this angle relates the parade to a vast urban landscape. The high angle also affords him the opportunity to convey movement into the parade. In this case the tracks of voice-over, visual texts and camera movements complement each other:

> And then also look at ways that I could not just select photos, but also like elements of photos that I took that would be really useful. And one of the things that I liked about this particular picture of the parade was the parade is centered really sort of low in the picture and there's sort of a lot of empty expanse of just sort of cityscape. And it was a great way to just sort of pan down to the parade as I was talking about discovering it. Because what really ended up happening was that just one morning below my hotel room I kind of looked down and, my God, there was a parade going on. So I think that that was a photograph that ended up even capturing that moment.

The meaning potentials of shot length and camera angles can be discussed with students drawing from conventions and language of film (for example, Golden, 2001). From such conventions, the long high-angle shot in this case could be dis-

cussed as setting up the scene, and perhaps even suggesting some initial separation between the viewer and the scene. Additionally, Gunther Kress and Theo
Van Leuwen (1996) have developed productive means of considering how hori-
zontal angles with respect to photographic subjects carry meaning, and also how
subjects are photographed as relatively objectified (in a position of 'offer' to the
viewer) or as directly engaging the viewer (in a position of 'demand').

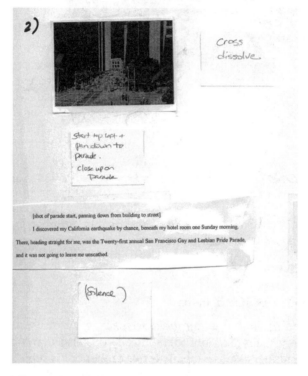

**Figure 9.5**  Todd's storyboard, frame 2

*Scene-building with images and playing with place and time*
As Todd re-mediates his print memoir into a multimedia story, not only does
he develop meanings through parallel media tracks, he also, visually, develops
the way in which he is producing scenes in the story and is transforming the
relations of space and time. While his earlier print memoir had only a fleeting
reference to there not being much of a gay community in Tennessee, in his digital story Todd sets up this contrast visually through two counter-posed scenes:
a photograph of the Bay Bridge that transitions into a photograph of a road
sign for 'The Other Side Club', a gay nightclub in rural Tennessee, which then
shifts to an image of the club building itself (Figure 9.6). When Todd set out to
visually represent the idea of the lack of a gay community in Tennessee, his
selected visuals developed into a short scene in the story, which itself prompted
him to develop his writing about Tennessee for use in his voice-over. The movements from print to visual and back to print generate new ideas. Moreover, in
having produced this new scene of the Other Side Club, we begin to see in this

example how the story begins to play with space and time, shifting from the narrator's present position in San Francisco, back to Tennessee, and returning to San Francisco again. While this is a small example, I have observed that my students seem much more prone to play with such space–time arrangements in composing when they are engaged in visual arrangement and other forms of media work than when they are not. Of course, this observation is not surprising, since a quality of film production has involved such play for decades.

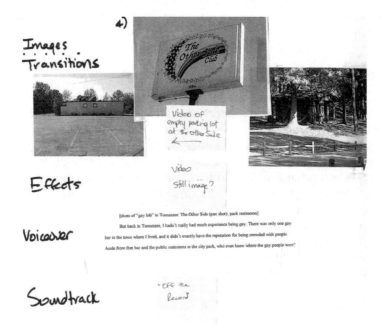

**Figure 9.6** Todd's storyboard, frame 3

*Contrasts through simultaneous images and texts*
As noted previously, Todd added new voice-over text to his digital story to tell us how to interpret the visual of Tennessee gay life, or the image of The Other Side Club:

> There was only one gay bar in the town where I lived, and it didn't exactly have the reputation for being crowded with people. Aside from that bar and the public restrooms in the city park, who even knew where the gay people were? (Figure 9.6)

An important characteristic of this print text is not merely that it runs parallel to the photograph, but that it develops an ironic relationship to it. Of course, one might interpret the tone of the print text alone ('exactly have the reputation …') as ironic, but the image, and the slow pan out from it across the empty parking lot, drive this point home with greater effect. Todd comments on others' responses to this ironic relationship of image to voice-over text and pan:

> I was sort of saying something really sarcastic about how it was always really crowded with people. That ended up drawing laughs in a way that I kind of expected it to because the timing just with my voiceover and then the pan out of the video worked really well.

This use of visuals and print (or other media) as sharply contrasting with one another, and leading to interpretations of irony, of gaps, of disagreement, of discordant voices, of humour or other, suggests a more advanced understanding of the simultaneous relationship of visuals to print text than is evident in the work of some students, who favour seeing one medium as necessarily illustrating or complementing the other.

## Conclusions

In literacy education, we find ourselves in a strange time period in which movements pull us in disparate directions. On the one hand, educators are under great pressure to ensure that all students can compose conventional academic prose for standardized assessments. On the other hand, many of the literacy practices that students engage in outside of school increasingly involve visuals and other media, and these practices seem increasingly remote from conventional academic prose. In this chapter, I offer an invitation to return to basic questions and bridging ways of thinking concerning composition. I argue that we need to back off from the products of composition, whether these are scholarly arguments, nature photographs, or musical scores, and consider thoughtfully how certain meta-level processes and dimensions of composition have powerful purchase across media. Using the case of composing personal memoir, I consider how personal memoir contains a number of dimensions that retain their importance and impact, regardless of media.

Through course description, lesson outlines, student work and student reflection, I illustrate how we might move toward a parallel pedagogy of 'old' print and 'new' non-print media, a pedagogy that I believe has benefits for present-day learning as well as for future literate practice. The examples given show something of how learning becomes powerful when it is driven by comparison and analogy, and when it is enacted across multiple forms of mediation. This kind of learning is restless and mobile, always seeking to understand one thing in terms of another; just as English grammar might be first understood through the study of French grammar, the print memoir is compared with the digital story, and the linguistic transition is understood through the visual transition. Of course, as discussed in the chapter, visuals and other media cannot be entirely understood or contained through their relations to print or other media. Yet, despite these limitations, the act of comparison itself helps us understand key distinctions between media types.

In addition to offering outcomes for immediate learning, ongoing movements towards parallel pedagogy could be promising for addressing some of the disparate demands that schools are facing. Indeed, it seems entirely untenable to imagine that essayist-based prose will be all that is needed for literacy success in work, leisure, and life pursuits in the 21st century. Yet, to take a stance of replacement of the old by the new, or of return to the old in rejection of the new is to ignore the repeated ways in which history has shown us how the old is absorbed and routinely transformed into new forms (Bolter and Grusin, 1999); we live within our history and beyond it, simultaneously. To deliberately juxtapose the old and new, then – print and pictures – might just make good pedagogic sense, as they seem to be continually chasing one another around anyway, concerned as they both are with telling a good story.

## References

Atwell, N. (1998) *In the Middle*. 2nd edn. Portsmouth, NH: Boynton/Cook.

Bakhtin, M.M. (1986) 'The problem of speech genres', trans. V.W. McGee, in C. Emerson and M. Holquist (eds), *Speech Genres and Other Late Essays*. Austin, TX: University of Texas Press.

Bolter, J. and Grusin, R. (1999) *Remediation: Understanding New Media*. Cambridge, MA: MIT Press.

Bruce, B.C. (1997) 'Literacy technologies: what stance should we take?', *Journal of Literacy Research*, 29(2): 289–309.

Gibson, J. (1979) *The Ecological Approach to Visual Perception*. Boston, MA: Houghton Mifflin.

Golden, J. (2001) *Reading in the Dark: Using Film as a Tool in the English Classroom*. Urbana, IL: National Council of Teachers of English.

Kinzer, C. and Leander, K. (2003) 'Reconsidering the technology/language arts divide: electronic and print-based environments', in D.L.D. Flood, J.R. Squire and J.M. Jensen (eds), *Handbook of Research on Teaching the English Language Arts*. Mahwah, NJ: Erlbaum. pp. 546–65.

Kist, W. (2005) *New Literacies in Action: Teaching and Learning in Multiple Media*. New York: Teachers College Press.

Kitchen, J. and Jones, M.P. (eds) (1999) *In Brief: Short Takes on the Personal*. New York: W.W. Norton.

Kress, G. and van Leeuwen, T. (1996) *Reading Images: The Grammar of Visual Design*. London: Routledge.

Lambert, J. (2002) *Digital Storytelling: Capturing Lives, Creating Community*. Berkeley, CA: Digital Diner Press.

Lankshear, C. and Knobel, M. (2003) *New Literacies: Changing Knowledge and Classroom Learning*. Philadelphia, PA: Open University Press.

Roorbach, B. (1998) *Writing Life Stories*. Cincinnati, OH: Story Press.

Smagorinski, P. (2002) *Teaching English through Principled Practice*. Upper Saddle River, NJ: Prentice Hall.

## Websites with digital story examples and information
**Capture Wales**
www.bbc.co.uk/wales/capturewales

**Center for Digital Storytelling**
www.storycenter.org
**City Voices, City Visions**
www.gse.buffalo.edu/org/cityvoices/productions.html
**Dana Atchley's Next Exit**
www.nextexit.com
**Design Examples and Communities**
www.bubbe.com, www.fray.com, www.links.net, www.alexrivera.com, http://
cultureisaweapon.org, www.creativenarrations.net, www.zonezero.com
**Digital Clubhouse Network**
www.digiclub.org
**Digital Storytelling Association**
www.dsaweb.org
**Digital Storytelling Festival**
www.dstory.com
**Hillary McLellan's Story Link**
http://tech-head.com/dstory.htm
(No stories here, but a good list of links to sites with other approaches to digital communication.)
**Silence Speaks**
www.silencespeaks.org/stories.html
**Stories of Service**
www.stories-of-service.org/theproject/
(Select 'See Our Work' near the bottom of the page.)

# Download

## Key points

1. 'New' media has features and dimensions of 'old' media within it, and these connections between new and old media can be a powerful tool for learning about multimedia production and interpretation.
2. In addition to connections between old and new media, particular media have certain affordances, or possibilities for functioning that allow them very different potentials to create effects and make meanings.
3. When students remediate messages from one medium to another they develop new understandings of their intended messages and different media.

## In your classroom

1. A common shortcoming of student experiments in new media production is that they focus on technical surface features at the expense of more meaningful generic qualities. In teaching multimedia production, it is helpful to go back to basic concepts of the genre you are working in and ask your students what makes that particular genre effective. For instance, good stories have a sense of a narrator's voice, no matter what media they appear in.
2. Using a language of 'composition' or 'design' across different media types, as well as compositional terms that readily traverse media (for example, 'big idea', 'transition', 'structure') can help your students develop a richer understanding of composing across media and building relations between simultaneous media.
3. Give students the opportunity to engage in observation, inquiry, comparison and synthesis concerning how particular dimensions of composition function in different media examples. Strive in this work to not give primacy to any medium, but rather to show the unique affordances of media types, as well as how particular composers and pieces make use of these affordances and simultaneous media.

## Further reading

Bolter, J. and Grusin, R. (1999) *Remediation: Understanding New Media.* Cambridge, MA: MIT Press.

Hull, G. and Nelson, M. (2005) 'Locating the semiotic power of multimodality', *Written Communication*, 22(2): 224–61.

Lambert, J. (2002) *Digital Storytelling: Capturing Lives, Creating Community.* Berkeley, CA: Digital Diner Press.

# Part D
## Interconnectivity

---

# Conclusion:
# Leaving Hong Kong

*Muriel Robinson and Victoria Carrington*

Our use of texts and the emergence of literacy is intimately entwined with the development of major cities. Print-based literacy grew out of the demands and needs of urban life and the availability of particular technologies, and it seems fitting that Hong Kong and cities like it – diverse, overcrowded, 24 hour – are laboratories for observing the emergence of new textual practices.

We believe that the divide often understood to exist between the material and the virtual is being remapped in places like Hong Kong and, in particular, in the lives and practices of young people in these sites. While heaving metropolises like Hong Kong, New York or Tokyo may be characterized as extreme or early adopters of new practices, these same practices can be seen in societies worldwide. Get on a train anywhere in the world and you will see combinations of mobile phones, iPods and other mp3 players, laptops, and hand-held gaming devices and interactive displays coexisting with static print as commuters engage with new texts and new digital spaces. Take a walk through any town centre or shopping mall and you will share the space with people who simultaneously inhabit physical and digital space as they walk and text, talk, upload and download on mobile phones.

It seems to us that networks, information and identities now flow back and forth across online and offline domains and, as a result, imagined communities and geographies operate in public spaces that are created and sustained by technology. Here we would make the point that all texts are produced and used within social contexts and are therefore deeply embedded in ways of living. Keeping this in mind, we suggest that new forms of technology are opening up public spaces where the work of individuals and groups can be circulated,

165

adding to the social and textual complexity of urban sites. It is in these new spaces that digital texts are coming into their own. These texts of social networking – games, blogs, wikis, Bebo, Cyworld and Facebook – are about creating and operating within complex new social spaces. Digital texts are the texts used to navigate, socialize, work and manoeuvre within these spaces. For many young people, the divide between on- and offline, often observed in the media and research, is a nonsense in terms of their lived experience across a range of social fields that include material and digital spaces. In turn, they require and have created forms of text that enable and support these lifestyles and needs.

The ability of individuals and groups to participate in a complex set of communities, to create and disseminate information, and to construct and transmit shared narratives in particular places is a core part of the life of an urban zone. As a consequence, digital culture and the texts that are created via digital technologies are increasingly embedded within these patterns of participation. The Hong Kong metro system is a case in point. As we travel across the city, our train carriage is full of people who are co-present. Their bodies may be in the train carriage with us but their social selves are elsewhere: they are immersed in hand-held games, movies and conversations, all of which require digital literacies and the digital technologies that produce and distribute digital texts. They are not using *just* text, nor are they using *just* a digital artefact, nor are they *just* using audio and visual cueing systems. They are using a new form of text to do both old and new things: to maintain important intimate relationships, to sustain connection to older forms of text by using new technology to access it, but also to read in new ways, to open up and make use of new social, political and economic spaces. Digital technologies and textual practices are deeply embedded in a city like Hong Kong because there is a social, political and economic space for them. New technologies and new practices with text emerge and become embedded only in concert with changes to prevailing cultural, economic and political infrastructure.

Of particular relevance to this publication is the synthesis evolving as printed and digital texts form and reform in a dialectic process that has meaning in its own right. Increasingly, the ability to work with and across print and digital forms of text, and to navigate their different affordances and applications, is a key skill for effective participation in the political and economic infrastructure of our societies (Jenkins et al., 2006). Mastery of printed literacy is necessary but no longer sufficient to guarantee individual and community participation. This rapid shift inevitably creates tension in classrooms steeped in generations of print-based literacy practices that are strongly linked to a particular moral and technological economy. The skills and attitudes that allow young people to develop these powerful masteries are not yet part of the explicit and formal classroom curriculum. Of course, there are deeply embedded historical and cultural reasons for the lag time between the emergence of digital technologies and digital literacy and their implementation in school-based curricula. However, as this book makes clear, there is a pressing need to engage meaningfully with what is, in effect, a new mainstream form of textual practice.

The contributors to this book have shown how a range of digital technologies and texts are now an everyday part of life outside classrooms for children and young people. These chapters foreground the ways in which new practices with digital text challenge older forms of authority in relation to knowledge production and expertise. They also highlight the ways in which important identity practices with these texts slide seamlessly back and forth between online and offline. These chapters challenge an older view of digital literacies as ancillary practices, and position them as key daily engagements with meaningful and powerful texts. Some of the chapters explore the extent to which the uses and affordances of such technologies by young people in everyday life are aligned, or not, with the ways in which schools approach new digital technologies and literacy education. In an era where these skills and texts are increasingly linked to employment, political access and the capacity to engage meaningfully in civic life, a literacy education that incorporates digital literacies is essential.

## Implications for teachers, both experienced and new

Importantly, one section of the book includes contributions that have taken a step further to consider the implications of these shifts for the ways in which our teacher preparation programmes operate across Australia, the UK and the USA. It is clear from these chapters, and from earlier studies (Honan, 2008; Robinson and Mackey, 2006), that not all prospective teachers are fully comfortable with new technologies or fully aware of the learning potential inherent in those which they do use with ease. The chapters in this volume have helped us to understand better the complexities of the situation and have clarified the need to support all prospective and existing teachers. Just as we need more reflection on practice by those still in classrooms, we also need to develop ways forward to assist those responsible for teacher education and to share the kinds of messages that Burnett, Kerin and Leander have to offer. This, we believe, is an important area of research and debate. Teachers need to have enough knowledge of how digital cultures, and out-of-school practices with digital technologies and digital literacies, are impacting on student learning; on student understandings and expectations of participation; and, crucially, the need to develop an approach to pedagogy that allows for shifting novice–expert relationships. We would make the case that preparing teachers to work in contemporary classrooms is a process of preparing them to be expert learners.

We believe that teachers should be prepared to move towards structuring class-rooms as learning communities where new knowledge is generated and distributed. In such a model, the role of the teacher will shift from conserving and transmitting already existing knowledge to helping students develop the skills and attitudes of expert learners (Carroll, 2000). As Carroll (2000) notes, recasting the classroom teacher in the role of *expert learner* would allow more scope to redefine the boundaries of learning. In this model, learning is not confined to the classroom but takes place across distributed networks using a range of technologies. There is also pedagogic space to recognize the online and offline learning, in and out of school, that contributes to the knowledge generation of the larger learning community. Dowdall and Davies make a convincing case for the importance of the complex literacies involved in out-of-school literacy practices with digital text and their relevance for educators. It follows, as Kerin, Burnett and Leander have demonstrated so well, that pre-service teacher preparation must respond to the challenges of digital literacies. We believe these chapters also demonstrate that fostering knowledge generation and collaborative learning communities is a step in the right direction.

In the opening chapter we suggested that the contentious technologies of everyday life posed some wicked issues for those of us in education – issues which resist straightforward and simplistic solutions but which need continued and careful study. Many of our contributors have indicated the challenges teachers face when finding ways to bring these technologies, and the many higher-level skills, competences and understandings that children have developed through their encounter with them, into the classroom context in a meaningful and appropriate way. We cannot pretend that these technologies do not bring with them highly contested narratives around issues such as violence, bullying and youth crime, although we can point to the lack of clear and reliable evidence as opposed to media hype. For example, at the time of writing, there has been a long-running story in the UK press about an alleged suicide pact among teenagers in a town in South Wales, supposedly supported and encouraged by their use of Bebo. Despite repeated statements by police and coroners that there is no evidence of any link (for example, *The Times* newspaper report by Dominic Kennedy, 2008) the story persists as an urban myth, and teachers, understandably, worry about using such social networking sites within their classrooms. Schools have tended to react to stories about phone theft, SMS bullying and mobile phone films of classrooms by banning phones or insisting they be turned off in class, and it is a brave beginning teacher who flies in the face of such established positions to explore, in a more thoughtful way, the potential of such technologies. Such, then, are the wicked issues that confront us as teachers and researchers, and which need considered and careful exploration by us all.

We hope that the examples within this book have offered some ideas and ways forward for readers seeking to develop their own practice. Just about every example in these chapters has started from a question asked by a teacher, teacher educator or researcher. Someone has watched what was going on, asked questions about it, and collected data or adapted their practice, or both, in order to reflect on what has happened. Although some of our case studies have been part of large funded research projects, others are much nearer to the kind of reflective practice that any teacher would support. It is important to note that even the largest funded projects have their origins in some earlier observation that has led to the construction of a research proposal. Teachers, through time and around the world, have been and remain in an ideal position to look at the evidence about the uses and affordances of digital technologies within the lives of their students. Each time a teacher reflects in this way, whether simply as part of ongoing reflection on how best to develop their pedagogy or as a spur to small- or large-scale action research, we gain deeper insight into digital cultures.

We hope that those of you reading this book nearer the beginning of your careers will continue the exploration of this territory through your own observation, teaching practice and reflection on outcomes. This cycle of observation, action and reflection is at the heart of action research methodology and, at the simplest level, is what happens every time a teacher thinks about what is happening in their classroom, adjusts their practice accordingly and then looks to see what difference this adjustment has made. This is not the place to begin to set out about the methods for more formal action research; there are many worthy volumes exploring action research methodology and plenty of master's courses available that support teachers to take their questions further and to add to the publicly available body of evidence. However, we would urge those who are contemplating undertaking a more formal piece of research not only to search out some support, but also to reflect back on the chapters in this book and what they have to offer as research models. As you revisit the chapters, and in particular the download sections where our contributors have tried to distil the essential messages of their work, we hope that you will reflect on your own experiences, in and out of the learning environment in which you work, and find questions which you want to explore in more depth.

Our own encounters with Hong Kong, where by chance we found ourselves while completing the work on this volume, reminded us of how much there is to consider about everyday uses of digital literacies. As a result, we leave Hong Kong with a greater insight into the ways in which new and old technologies and practices with text coexist, compete and evolve into something new. Any journey on public transport or shopping trip to a city centre offers similar opportunities to see what young people are doing, as does any conversation with students in schools and universities. We believe that we need to use such opportunities to understand how the world of the classroom might need to change and adapt to reflect more fully the world beyond the classroom walls. Our contributors have shown us what they have found out, but the story is far from over, and we hope that this book will inspire at least some of its readers to add to the narrative through their own research in this area.

## References

Carroll, T.G. (2000) 'If we didn't have the schools we have today, would we create the schools we have today?', *Contemporary Issues in Technology and Teacher Education*, 1(1). Retrieved 27 August 2008, from www.citejournal.org/vol1/iss1/currentissues/general/article1.htm

Honan, E. (2008) 'Barriers to teachers using digital texts in literacy classrooms', *Literacy*, 42(1): 36–43.

Jenkins, H., Clinton, K., Purushotma, R., Robison, A. and Weigel, M. (2006) *Confronting the Challenges of Participatory Culture: Media Education for the 21st Century*. Chicago, IL: The John D and Catherine T MacArthur Foundation.

Kennedy, D. (2008) 'No suicide pact, say police after another teenager is found hanged in Bridgend', *Times Online*. Retrieved 21 April 2008, from www.timesonline.co.uk/tol/news/uk/article3784277.ece

Robinson, M. and Mackey, M. (2006) 'Assets in the classroom: comfort and competence with media among teachers present and future', in J. Marsh and E. Millard (eds), *Popular Literacies, Childhood and Schooling*. London: Routledge. pp. 200–20.

# Index